THE
WISDOM
OF THE
ANCIENTS:
Mining the Riches
of Genesis 1 - 11

S T E V E   L A N G F O R D

Print information available on the last page.

ISBN: 978-1-6987-0783-9 (sc)
ISBN: 978-1-6987-0781-5 (hc)
ISBN: 978-1-6987-0782-2 (e)

Library of Congress Control Number: 2021911478

Trafford rev. 06/21/2021

Trafford PUBLISHING® www.trafford.com

North America & international
toll-free: 844-688-6899 (USA & Canada)
fax: 812 355 4082

CONTENTS

THE STORY OF CAIN
Genesis 4:1—26

FROM ADAM TO NOAH: A GENEALOGICAL BRIDGE
Genesis 5:1—32

THE STORY OF NOAH AND THE FLOOD
Genesis 6:1—9:29

REPOPULATING THE EARTH: THE GENEALOGICAL TABLE OF NOAH
Genesis 10

THE STORY OF THE TOWER OF BABEL
Genesis 11:1—9

FROM THE TOWER OF BABEL TO ABRAM:
THE GENEALOGICAL BRIDGE OF SHEM
Genesis 11:10—32

INTRODUCTION

D id God create the world in seven literal days? Where was the Garden of Eden? Were Adam and Eve really the first man and woman? Where did Cain get his wife? Did people really live to be hundreds of years old back then? Did God really destroy the world with a flood?

These are the kinds of questions that surface when people read the great narratives found in Genesis 1—11. They are questions that probe the historical character of the stories. Each is asking, "Were these stories actual historical events?"

Some Christians find these questions offensive. For them, the Bible is totally reliable, without question. If it's what the Bible says, it's true. End of story.

But, for others, these questions persist, waiting for an answer. They are honest questions that grow out of how we have been trained to think.

Our thinking is shaped by two cultural influences: science and reason. Science is the attempt to understand and explain our natural world using observation, study, testing, and logic. It seeks to identify verifiable facts that we can believe as true. Reason is the companion of science. It is the kind of thinking we use to determine what is true. Our reliance upon reason is the product of the Enlightenment.[1] Both of these influences lie outside our awareness. They are simply the way we naturally think. They are how we in the modern world have been trained to think.

Naturally, these two influences impact how we read the Bible. We read, looking for facts to believe. We read, using reason to question what we read. So the questions that arise as we read these early chapters of Genesis—and the rest of the Bible, as well—are Western, scientifically oriented questions. They are questions that grow out of our ability to reason. They are questions about the facts of the stories. Are the stories accurate? Can we believe them as true?

The problem with our questions—if there is one—is that we are asking Western, scientifically-oriented questions of ancient material which came from Near East cultures. These ancient texts were written from a prescientific perspective. Each of these traits—ancient, Near Eastern, prescientific—is an important factor in our effort to understand these stories.

The ancient Hebrews, rather than using science to explain those aspects of life they did not understand, explained them in theological or spiritual terms. They viewed them as the work of gods or spirits, particularly evil spirits.

The primary way they communicated their understandings was by telling stories. They used stories to communicate from one generation to the next the spiritual truths they knew. Their stories were the vehicles they used to transmit their spiritual understanding. Thus, storytelling was a key component of their culture.

So we face a major challenge when we read the Bible. Everything we find in the Bible is ancient, Near Eastern, and prescientific in its orientation while our orientation is Western, scientific, and reason-based.

We, the readers	The biblical authors
Western	Near Eastern
Scientifically-oriented, reason-based thinking	Prescientific, theologically oriented thinking
Modern and Post-modern	Ancient

This contrast leads us to ask the wrong kind of questions. We ask Western questions of Near Eastern stories. We ask questions the authors never anticipated. We ask questions the Bible does not answer.

The questions we ask determine the answers we find and the conclusions we reach. Asking a question the text does not answer leads us into speculation and to pointless arguments that do nothing to nurture our spiritual lives.[2] More significantly, asking a question the text does not answer leads us away from what the author was intending to say. We miss the truth the story teaches—truth intended to nurture our spiritual lives.

Our Western, scientifically-oriented thinking leads us to focus on the details of the story—the vehicle that carries the deeper understanding. While we would like to have answers to our Western, scientifically-oriented questions, it is more important for us to understand what the author was communicating. Our objective is to understand the spiritual truth the authors wanted us to know. This objective calls us to set aside our questions about the details of the story in order to ask different questions: what spiritual truth was the biblical writer attempting to communicate? What theological truth does this story contain? What does this story tell us about life, about ourselves, about God? These questions position us to let the text say what it was intended to say. While answering our Western, scientifically-oriented questions may satisfy our curiosity, learning the spiritual truth the biblical text contains has the potential to shape our lives.

This book approaches these ancient texts as stories originally told to communicate spiritual understanding rather than to relate historical events. It views these narratives as great theological statements reflecting the early Hebrews' understanding of God, creation, us humans, their nation, life, and the relationship that ties them together. These stories and the spiritual truths they communicate are foundational to the identity of the people of Israel. This book seeks to probe their understanding, reclaiming the insights the stories offer. It moves beyond the questions we commonly ask of these stories— Western, scientifically-oriented, reason-based questions—in order to probe the wisdom these ancient narratives offer.

CHAPTER 1

INTRODUCING GENESIS 1–11

The first eleven chapters of Genesis are composed of five great narratives:

- the creation story—when God spoke creation into being (Genesis 1:1—2:3)
- the story of the garden (Genesis 2—3),
- the story of Cain (Genesis 4),
- the story of Noah and the flood (Genesis 6—9),
- the story of the tower of Babel (Genesis 11:1—9).

The first story is a beautifully crafted poetic narrative about creation that was written during the nation's experience of exile in Babylon, sometime after 586 B.C.E. The other four were originally a part of the oral history of the Hebrew people. They were passed down by word of mouth from generation to generation until the time they were written down.

These five narratives are woven together by three genealogical tables. The first genealogy links the story of Adam to the story of Noah. The second links the story of Noah to the story of the tower of Babel. The final genealogy links the story of the tower of Babel to the story of Abram, the forefather of the nation of Israel. But these genealogies are more than ways of linking the stories together. They are part of the stories, growing out of the previous story and providing the setting for the next story. They help to advance the larger story being told in Genesis 1—11. These connecting links indicate these stories are not isolated stories that stand alone. They are interrelated and interconnected.

The focus of these epic narratives is humankind in general. They are a part of what is called primeval history. That means they occurred before recorded history. That is why they were passed down orally from generation to generation. At Genesis 11:27, the focus of the narrative shifts from humankind in general to one specific family—the family of Abram (Abraham) whose descendants became the nation of Israel. Beginning with Genesis 11:27, the biblical materials deal with places and cities that can be identified historically.

These narratives set the backdrop to the story of the nation of Israel. They provide a theological framework that undergirds the nation's identity. They would have been read by the people of Israel as a part of their story.

The stories reflect the hand of an editor who used material from multiple sources to compose the narrative. The editor's work is evident in the repeated use of the formula "these are the generations of." This formula is used ten different times in the book of Genesis, each time indicating a shift in the story. It reflects the editor's outline of the book. "These are the generations of" ...

- the heavens and the earth, Genesis 2:4
- Adam, Genesis 5:1
- Noah, Genesis 6:9
- Shem, Ham, and Japheth, Genesis 10:1
- Shem, Genesis 11:10
- Terah, Genesis 11:27
- Ishmael, Genesis 25:12
- Isaac, Genesis 25:19
- Esau, Genesis 36:1
- Jacob, Genesis 37:2.

The book of Genesis is a part of a larger unit consisting of the first five books of the Bible: Genesis, Exodus, Leviticus, Numbers, Deuteronomy. This larger unit is known as the Pentateuch.[3] For the Hebrew people, they are known as the Torah or the Law. These books tell the story of the people of Israel, beginning with creation, till the time they prepared to enter the Land of Promise. The editor of Genesis was involved in editing this larger unit, as well.

The sources the editor used can be identified in two ways: (1) the underlying interests reflected in the stories and (2) in the names for God that are used in the stories. A primary source is associated with the name *Yahweh* (YWH), commonly translated as the LORD. The stories from this source are associated with the southern kingdom of Judah. They have a strong interest in the covenant the LORD made with the people at Mt. Sinai. Stories from the northern kingdom of Israel commonly use the name *Elohim* when speaking of God. This name is translated simply as God. Some stories reflect an interest in things related to the priests and their role. See, for example, Genesis 2:1—3 and 7:1—5. These stories come from a priestly source. A final source is tied to the book of Deuteronomy and its theology.

The Pentateuch—along with the other parts of Hebrew Scripture—was compiled during the time of the Exile. This collecting and compiling of their national story was a way the Hebrew people sought to reclaim their identity after the historical basis of their identity—their nation and king, their capital city of Jerusalem, and their Temple—had been destroyed by the armies of Babylon in 586 B.C.E.

THE STORY OF CREATION

Genesis 1:1—2:3

Genesis 1:1–2:3 (NRSV)[4]

I n the beginning when God created the heavens and the earth, [2]the earth was a formless void and darkness covered the face of the deep, while a wind from God swept over the face of the waters.

[3]Then God said, "Let there be light"; and there was light. [4]And God saw that the light was good; and God separated the light from the darkness. [5]God called the light Day, and the darkness he called Night. And there was evening and there was morning, the first day.

[6]And God said, "Let there be a dome in the midst of the waters, and let it separate the waters from the waters." [7]So God made the dome and separated the waters that were under the dome from the waters that were above the dome. And it was so. [8]God called the dome Sky. And there was evening and there was morning, the second day.

[9]And God said, "Let the waters under the sky be gathered together into one place, and let the dry land appear." And it was so. [10]God called the dry land Earth, and the waters that were gathered together he called Seas. And God saw that it was good. [11]Then God said, "Let the earth put forth vegetation: plants yielding seed, and fruit trees of every kind on earth that bear fruit with the seed in it." And it was so. [12]The earth brought forth vegetation: plants yielding seed of every kind, and trees of every kind bearing fruit with the seed in it. And God saw that it was good. [13]And there was evening and there was morning, the third day.

[14]And God said, "Let there be lights in the dome of the sky to separate the day from the night; and let them be for signs and for seasons and for days and years, [15]and let them be lights in the dome of the sky to give light upon the earth." And it was so. [16]God made the two great lights—the greater light to rule the day and the lesser light to rule the night—and the stars. [17]God set them in the dome of the sky to give light upon the earth, [18]to rule over the day and over the night, and to separate the light from the darkness. And God saw that it was good. [19]And there was evening and there was morning, the fourth day.

[20]And God said, "Let the waters bring forth swarms of living creatures, and let birds fly above the earth across the dome of the sky." [21]So God created the great sea monsters and every living creature that moves, of every kind, with which the waters swarm, and every winged bird of every kind. And God saw that it was good. [22]God blessed them, saying, "Be fruitful and multiply and fill the waters in the seas, and let

birds multiply on the earth." [23]And there was evening and there was morning, the fifth day.

[24]And God said, "Let the earth bring forth living creatures of every kind: cattle and creeping things and wild animals of the earth of every kind." And it was so. [25]God made the wild animals of the earth of every kind, and the cattle of every kind, and everything that creeps upon the ground of every kind. And God saw that it was good.

[26]Then God said, "Let us make humankind in our image, according to our likeness; and let them have dominion over the fish of the sea, and over the birds of the air, and over the cattle, and over all the wild animals of the earth, and over every creeping thing that creeps upon the earth." [27]So God created humankind in his image, in the image of God he created them; male and female he created them. [28]God blessed them, and God said to them, "Be fruitful and multiply, and fill the earth and subdue it; and have dominion over the fish of the sea and over the birds of the air and over every living thing that moves upon the earth."

[29]God said, "See, I have given you every plant yielding seed that is upon the face of all the earth, and every tree with seed in its fruit; you shall have them for food. [30]And to every beast of the earth, and to every bird of the air, and to everything that creeps on the earth, everything that has the breath of life, I have given every green plant for food." And it was so.

[31]God saw everything that he had made, and indeed, it was very good. And there was evening and there was morning, the sixth day.

Thus the heavens and the earth were finished, and all their multitude. [2]And on the seventh day God finished the work that he had done, and he rested on the seventh day from all the work that he had done. [3]So God blessed the seventh day and hallowed it, because on it God rested from all the work that he had done in creation.

CHAPTER 2

THE CREATION STORY

Did God create the world in seven days?

We will not pursue this common question so that it does not divert us from our objective: identifying the spiritual understanding the creation story communicates. Instead, we will pursue a different question: what truth did the biblical writer want to communicate in describing the creation of the world?

Our quest begins by looking at what the creation story actually says.

When God Spoke Creation into Being

The creation story is a beautifully crafted, intricately designed narrative. It is poetic in nature.[5] Hebrew parallelism—an essential characteristic of Hebrew poetry—lies at the core of its structure.[6]

The story divides naturally into 3 sections:

- 1:1—2, an introductory description of the earth as God began creating.
- 1:3—31, the six days of creation in which God spoke the world into being.
- 2:1—3, the concluding seventh day in which God rested.

<u>1:1—2, introductory description of the earth as God began creating</u>

"In the beginning when God created the heavens and the earth" (Genesis 1:1). God's shaping the earth was a part of God's larger work of creating the universe. The phrase "the heavens and the earth" (verse 1) is the Hebrew way of speaking of the universe—all that is.

Two phrases describe the condition of the earth before God began working with it. At this stage, the earth was like the lump of clay a potter throws on the potter's wheel before beginning to fashion the clay into the shape he has in mind.

The earth was described as "a formless void," 1:1. This first phrase translates two Hebrew adjectives: formless and void. *Formless* communicates the idea of being without shape, structure, or form. The Hebrew adjective *void* —translated by the NRSV as a noun—means empty, without content. The idea was the earth, before God began to fashion it, was an empty, shapeless glob. These two descriptors provide the key to understanding the next portion of the story—the six days of creation. In the six days of creation, God addressed and reversed this twofold condition. God brought structure and order to that which was formless. Then God filled with abundance that which was empty or void.

The second phrase used to describe the earth at this stage is "darkness covered the face of the deep." Again, the phrase incorporates two images: darkness and water. Darkness and water covered the face or the surface of the earth. These two images carried meaning the Hebrew people would understand. The ancient Hebrews viewed the sea as a power they could not control and as a power that would destroy them were they to venture onto it. Thus, "the waters" and "the deep" were terms they used to speak of power that destroys. They were metaphors used to speak of chaos and evil. Similarly, the ancient Hebrews viewed darkness as the realm of evil, the time when evil doers were active. We see both of these concepts in the book of Job. Job 38:8—11 speaks of God's authority over evil by describing the limits God put on the sea:

> Or who shut in the sea with doors when it burst out from the womb?
> —when I made the clouds its garment, and thick darkness its swaddling band,
> and prescribed bounds for it, and set bars and doors,
> and said, 'Thus far shall you come, and no farther,
> and here shall your proud waves be stopped'?

God's authority over evil is also expressed in Job 38:12—15 where the morning light drives away the darkness, taking away the cover of darkness in which the wicked operate. These two images—deep, darkness—describe the condition of the earth at this stage as being overshadowed by chaos and evil.

God's presence and work in this situation is referenced in a third phrase: "a wind from God swept over the face of the waters," Genesis1:2. In spite of the earth's formless emptiness, in spite of it being overshadowed by chaos and evil, God was not absent. The Hebrew word translated as "wind" can also be translated as breath or spirit. So this single phrase can mean a wind of God or the breath of God or the Spirit of God. God's wind-breath-Spirit moved across the surface of the watery, dark chaos. The six days of creation repeatedly use the phrase "and God said." Linking that phrase with "a wind from God," we could say "a God-breathed whisper moved across the face of the earth's chaos like a gentle wind." God was at work in the midst of the chaos and evil.

The beginning of God's work in shaping the earth was in the Spirit's (or wind's) movement across the face of the deep.

1:3—31, the six days of creation in which God spoke creation into being

The heart of the creation story is the six days of creation in which God spoke creation into being. This section of the narrative has two dominant features, both of which are characteristic of Hebrew poetry. These two features give the narrative its poetic flavor.

The first feature is a pattern that is repeated in each of the six days:

- And God said.
- And it was so.
- And God saw that it was good (in days three through six).
- And there was evening and there was morning, the first (or second or third, etc.) day.

No part of this pattern is found in the account of the seventh day.

God created by simply speaking: "let there be" and "let the." God envisioned each aspect of creation, and then put that vision into words. What God envisioned, God spoke. What God spoke came into being. "And it was so."

Each dimension of God's creative work is associated with a particular day of the week, designated by the phrase "and there was evening and there was morning." Evening and morning reflect the Hebrew understanding that the day began at sundown—evening—as opposed to the Western view that the day begins with the sunrise or the scientific view that the day begins at midnight. The week, marked off by the Sabbath, was the central unit of time for the Hebrew people. The author structured the creation narrative around their concept of a week.

The second feature of the six days of creation is Hebrew parallelism. While the repeated pattern of each day is easily identified, parallelism is found in the relationship between the first three days and the last three days. (See below.) In the six days of creation, God addressed and reversed the earth's condition as a "formless void" (verse 2).

In the first three days of creation, God addressed the formless condition of the earth. God spoke boundaries and structure into creation by creating separation and distinctions within the earth's watery darkness.

The first day of creation (Genesis 1:3—5) On the first day, God dealt with the darkness that covered the face of the deep. God said, "Let there be light," (verse 3). God separated the light from the darkness, creating a distinction between the two. God named the light Day and the darkness Night (verse 5). "And there was evening and there was morning, the first day" (verse 5).

The second day of creation (Genesis 1:6—8) Having dealt with the darkness that covered the watery surface of the earth, God then addressed the watery surface itself. God spoke, creating a dome in the midst of the waters. God called the dome Sky (verse 8). The waters were separated into those above the dome and those below it. "And there was evening and there was morning, the second day" (verse 8).

The third day of creation (Genesis 1:9—13) Once again, God dealt with the watery surface of the earth. God spoke, creating a separation in the waters below the dome so that dry land appeared. God called the dry land Earth and the waters Seas (verse 10.) For the first time, the story adds, "And God saw that it was good" (verse 10). Rather than moving to "and there was evening and there was morning, the third day," the author inserted an additional detail. God spoke a second time, bringing forth a second creative act on this third day. This second creative act caused the earth to produce fruits and plants of every kind (verse 11—12). Once again, the author noted "God saw that it was good" (verse 13). "And there was evening and there was morning, the third day" (verse 13).

In these first three days, God reversed the earth's formless condition by creating a distinction between light and darkness, between the sky and the seas, and between the dry land and the sea. God gave the earth structure and form.

In the next three days, God addressed the earth's emptiness. At this point, Hebrew parallelism comes into play. The last three days are tied to the first three. What was given shape on the first day (light and darkness) was filled on <u>the fourth day of creation</u> with the sun, moon, and the stars (Genesis 1:14—19). What was given shape on the second day (the sky, the seas) was filled on <u>the fifth day of creation</u> with birds for the sky and fish for the seas (Genesis 1:20—23). What was given shape on the third day (the dry land and the seas) was filled on <u>the sixth day of creation</u> with the cattle and wild animals to populate the dry land along with the creation of humankind in God's image to rule over them (Genesis 1:24—31).

<u>Formless</u>	<u>Void (Empty)</u>
Day 1—light and darkness	Day 4—sun, moon, and stars
Day 2—the sky and the seas	Day 5—the birds of the sky, the fish of the seas
Day 3—the dry land	Day 6—the cattle and wild animals, humankind

In the six days of creation, God addressed the formlessness and the emptiness of the earth's original condition, shaping it in the first three days, filling it in the last three.

<u>2:1—3, the seventh day in which God rested</u>

The creation of humankind in God's image to rule over creation marked the end of God's creating work. Having finished the work, God rested. God stopped working ... at the task of creating the earth! God's rest does not mean God stopped working. Having completed the task of creating the heavens and the earth, God moved to a different kind of work. God moved to the task of bringing creation to its intended end—maturity. God is now at work nurturing all of creation—especially us humans—into a maturity that reflects the divine likeness in which we were created.

The seventh day was blessed because God rested on it from the work of creating. God's rest underscores the importance of the Sabbath for the Hebrew people. This reference to the seventh day suggests a priestly source for this story of creation.

A Guide for Personal Reflection and Journaling, for Group Conversation and Discussion

1. What new thought or understanding did you have about the story of creation?
2. How does that new thought or understanding impact the way you read the story?

CHAPTER 3

THE CREATION STORY AS A MESSAGE OF HOPE AND POLITICAL DEFIANCE

T his carefully designed narrative was not crafted to say something as simple as "God created the world." Nor was it designed to assert that God created the world in seven literal days as so many today insist. (Actually, the text indicates that creation was finished in six days, not seven—if you read it literally.) The author designed it to communicate a word of encouragement and hope in the face of the challenges his audience was facing. Like each of the five narratives found in Genesis 1—11, it was designed to speak to the spiritual lives of the people. As such, it speaks to ours, as well.

A Message of Hope

This creation narrative was written late in Israel's history, during their exile experience in Babylon. In 586 B.C.E., the armies of Babylon overran the city of Jerusalem. They destroyed the city and the Temple. They took the king and his court captive, bringing the nation to an end. They carried the king, his court, and the majority of the people away to Babylon where they were forced to live in exile.

The lives of the Hebrew people were turned upside down by their experience of exile. Everything that shaped their lives and gave them meaning—family, homes, land passed down through generations, businesses, the Temple and the covenant with God, the king and the nation itself—was taken from them, destroyed by the hand of an invading nation. They struggled to rebuild their lives in the midst of the strange ways of a foreign land. Every day was lived under the heavy hand of the hostile power that had robbed them of everything they treasured. They lived under a dark cloud of loss and grief.

The devastation they experienced created a major theological crisis in their lives. They felt abandoned by the LORD, forsaken and forgotten. The covenant upon which their identity was founded seemed to be a thing of the past. The Temple which was the focal point of their religious life was destroyed and, with it, their sense of connection with the LORD. Their spiritual lives were filled with darkness as they questioned why God let such a thing happen to them. Little was left upon which to rebuild their lives, much less to give them meaning.

One could say their situation was like the condition of the world before God began to speak into it: formless—robbed of everything around which they had built their lives and their sense of identity, empty—robbed of everything that gave their lives a sense of meaning and purpose, full of chaos as they were faced with rebuilding their lives without the theological foundations of their past, overshadowed by evil and darkness.

This kind of life experience is the one for which the creation narrative was penned. This poetic narrative was a reminder that—in the midst of their chaos and destruction, in the midst of their emptiness and darkness—God was at work. A wind from God—the whispering breath of God—the Spirit of God was blowing across the face of their exile experience. God was calling forth light in their darkness, order in their chaos, and life that was good to fill their emptiness. God was at work bringing life out of their experience of death—what the New Testament calls resurrection.

This creation narrative does indeed affirm that God is the creator of the world. But it declares so much more about God. It affirms God's authority over chaos and evil. Our experiences of chaos and evil in life are never the final word. God is always at work, moving over the face of the chaos, speaking into it to reverse it, bringing forth life and that which is good. The narrative affirms how God uses power. God always uses power in life-giving, life-enriching ways. God never uses power to destroy. Even in dealing with chaos and evil, God does not attack it to destroy it. Rather, God moves over its surface. God speaks into it. God transforms it. God reverses its life-depleting impact. God always works to bring forth that which is good and filled with abundance.

This carefully designed poem stirs hope in the face of hopelessness. It calls for faith in the midst of those times that cause us to question our faith. It calls for perseverance when we feel like giving up. It calls for patience when we wonder "what's the use?" It calls for faithfulness when it would be easier to give in to our pain, despondency, and depression.

But this poetic narrative does not just tell us something about God. It also tells us something about who we are, as well.

A Work of Political Defiance

The creation of each of the six days of creation followed the same repeated pattern (as we saw above):

- And God said.
- And it was so.
- And God saw that it was good (in days three through six).
- And there was evening and there was morning, the first (or second or third, etc.) day.

The only variation in this pattern occurs on days three and six. That variation is designed to catch our attention. It shines a spotlight on what occurs, especially on the sixth day.

The third day has two variations. On the third day, God separated the waters beneath the sky, causing dry ground to appear. God called the dry land Earth while the waters were called Seas. At this point, a new element—the first variation—is introduced into the pattern: "And God saw that it was good" (Genesis 1:10). The structure that God had brought to the formless condition of the earth—light and darkness, sky above and waters below, dry land and the seas—was seen as "good." A second variation in the pattern then occurs. On days one, two, four, and five, only one act of creation took place. But on this third day (and again on the sixth), a second act of creation took place. Having brought forth the dry ground, God spoke a second time so that the dry ground brought forth vegetation—plants and fruit trees. Once again, "God saw that it was good" (Genesis 1:12). It seems these two variations point to the goodness of what God had created, especially the productivity of the land.

The sixth day duplicates the variations of the third day. God spoke twice, the first time creating domesticated and wild animals (Genesis 1:24—25), the second time creating humankind (Genesis 1:26-27). The two-fold affirmation of "it was good" is repeated with a significant change. After the creation of humankind, "God saw everything he had made, and indeed, it was *very good*" (Genesis 1:31, emphasis added).

The variations of the sixth day indicate the creation of humankind was a major point—if not *the* major point—of the creation story. The significance of humankind is underscored in three ways. Humans—both male and female—were created in God's image and likeness (Genesis 1:27). They were given authority to rule over all living things (Genesis 1:28). Finally, after their creation, God declared all of creation "very good" (Genesis 1:31). The creation of human in God's likeness made creation not just good, but very good. We humans were the crowning touch that made everything complete. The creation of humankind in the image and likeness of God is the high point of the creation story.

In order to understand the author's emphasis, we need to understand the backdrop against which his narrative was written.

We know the creation narrative was written during the Hebrew people's experience of Babylonian captivity. One dimension of that experience sheds light on the author's emphasis upon our being created in the image and likeness of God.

Every year, the Babylonians celebrated the beginning of their new year by retelling their creation story. Their story was one of the oldest, if not the oldest, creation story in existence. It first appeared in written form about 1100 B.C.E., etched on seven stone tablets. It likely existed in oral form long before that. The Babylonian version—known as *Enuma Elish*—is but one version of this Mesopotamian creation myth. Marduk, the god of Babylon, is the hero in the Babylonian version.

The story begins with waters swirling around in chaos. Creation came into being as the waters separated into fresh water and salt water. The fresh water was known as the god Apsu while the salt water was known as the goddess Tiamat. From these two gods, other lesser gods were born.

In the story, the lesser, younger gods were like rambunctious children. Their play disturbed Apsu, making it impossible for him to sleep at night and disrupting his work during the day. In his frustration, he turned to his adviser for counsel. He was advised to get rid of those who were disturbing his peace. Apsu agreed with the advisor's counsel and planned to kill the lesser gods. Tiamat learned of his plan and warned her eldest son, Enki (also known as Ea). Enki then killed Apsu while he slept. Enki celebrated by using Apsu's body to create a house in which to live.

After Apsu's death, Tiamat turned on the lesser gods. Seeking revenge for her mate's death, she summoned the forces of chaos, creating eleven monsters to attack her offspring. Enki led the younger gods in fighting Tiamat and her forces, but were unable to prevail against them. When all seemed lost, the youngest god—Marduk— captured Tiamat's general, Quingu. Then, using a net, Marduk caught Tiamat who had taken the form of a huge sea monster or dragon. He drove an evil wind down her throat, then shot her with an arrow. The arrow pierced her heart and caused her bloated stomach to explode. Marduk used her body to create the heavens and the earth. From her two eyes flowed the Tigris and the Euphrates Rivers.

Now victorious, Marduk assumed the position of chief god with undisputed power. The other lesser gods, fearing his wrath, agreed. He assigned the lesser gods roles to play in his new creation. He also imprisoned those who had maintained loyalty to Tiamat. Among those imprisoned was Tiamat's general, Quingu. Marduk, working with his older brother Enkia (Ea), killed Quingu, the general. Ea used Quingu's blood to create the first man. The man was created to help the gods maintain order and keep chaos at bay.

In this creation story, both the universe and human beings were created out of acts of violence. Humans were created to maintain order by using power violently to destroy the enemy. In this story, war was the way to peace. The order gained through violence was maintained through a hierarchy that continued the pattern of domination. The king, as the representative of the god Marduk, was the head of that hierarchy. He was divinely appointed to maintain order by using power against those who opposed his authority. In this hierarchy, those without power or standing served those with power. Those with power were the important ones. Everyone else was insignificant. They were only there to serve those in power.

Every new year, the Babylonian creation story was reenacted in a New Year's Day Tournament of Roses-like parade. The Hanging Gardens of Babylon—one of the seven wonders of the ancient world—were the temple of the god Marduk and the location of the reenactment. The king played the role of Marduk, the hero. This annual ritual reestablished the king's right to rule, using force when necessary, and reinforced the order that grew out of his control.

In the face of this annual reenactment, an unidentified Hebrew poet-prophet penned the Genesis 1 creation story: "in the beginning when God created the heavens and the earth." The Hebrew creation account proclaimed a vastly different understanding of God, of creation, of life, and of human beings. Compare the two.

In the Babylonian creation story, violence was a part of the nature of their gods. The gods used their power to destroy those they viewed as a threat or an enemy. Violence and evil were an inherent part of creation and an inherent part of human beings.

In the biblical creation story, God used divine power to create that which was good, not to dominate or destroy. God brought forth light and life, gave shape to that which was formless, and filled that which was empty and void. God used power on behalf of, not against; for the good of, not to destroy. And that which God created was good, very good.

In the Babylonian creation story, domination of the other was the heart of the story. Order was achieved by using power against the other, to eliminate the threat. War—defeating and destroying the enemy—was seen as the way to peace. Peace was defined as stability. Order—or stability—was maintained by those in power, in the positions at the top of the hierarchy. Domination was the means by which peace and stability were maintained.

In the biblical creation story, domination of the other has no place. Order came through the spoken word: "and God said." God worked in the midst of chaos as the wind-breath-Spirit of God moved over the face of the deep. God's power was expressed through the creative word that clarified and identified differences. God's word created a place for the light and the darkness, the waters above and the waters below, dry land and the seas. When each had their place, they could be filled with abundance and life. Creation came out of chaos through the power of the word. Truth that honors and finds a place for both sides was the way out of the chaos of conflict.

In the Babylonian creation story, human beings were the product of violence, created from the blood of an executed lesser god. Evil and violence are in our blood. They are a part of our DNA.

In the biblical creation story, humans are created in the image of God. They were created for God's kind of life. They, like God, have creative powers that can be used for good.

In the Babylonian creation story, the villain was female, the mother goddess Tiamat. Her fury created the threat to the lesser gods' lives. She had to be defeated for there to be stability and peace. She had to be conquered by a male. The unspoken message in this depiction was that women are evil. They have to be controlled. A man's power and control are needed for stability.

In the biblical creation story, both male and female were created in the image of God. Both were created for God's kind of life. Both possess the power to be creative.

The biblical story of creation presents a vastly different understanding than does the Babylonian creation story—a different understanding of God, of life, of who we are as humans, of women, of how power is used. The biblical story challenged the commonly accepted way of thinking and living in the Babylonian world in which they were exiled. It was a call to think and live differently. It was a work of political defiance.

In a world rated R for violence, what spiritual truth might this Hebrew story of creation have for us?

A Guide for Personal Reflection and Journaling, for Group Conversation and Discussion

1. How does the understanding of the backdrop to the story presented in this chapter change how you read the story?
2. When have you experienced a situation that robbed you of hope? How does the creation story speak to that experience?
3. What is your reaction to the idea that the Genesis 1 creation story is an act of political defiance?
4. What parts of our culture might be challenged by the truths presented in the story of creation?

CHAPTER 4

IN THE IMAGE OF GOD

What does it mean that we have been created in God's image, according to God's likeness? Two phrases in the text give us a clue: "and let them have dominion over," (Genesis 1:26); "fill the earth and subdue it; and have dominion over" (Genesis 1:28).

These two words—subdue, dominion—speak of the use of power. "Subdue" carries the image of overpowering and conquering—using power against the other in order to control them. To "have dominion over" expresses the same thought—power over. Power used against the other is the heart of the Babylonian creation story.

A bit of reflection, however, leads us to a different understanding of these terms in the creation story.

God subdued the chaos that characterized the earth before God began to work with it. But God did not subdue the chaos by using power against it. Rather, God worked in the midst of the chaos, moving over the face of it. God spoke into the formless void of chaos, bringing forth that which was good. The wind-breath-Spirit of God moved across the face of the waters of chaos, calling forth form and structure to that which was formless (the first three days of creation) and filling that which was empty with that which was good (the final three days of creation).

The Hebrew word translated as "dominion over" carries a different image than power over. The word communicates the concept "to orchestrate." God created humankind to bring all the pieces of creation into harmony—each in its proper place, contributing its unique gift, working together to produce that which was very good. We humans were created to be the conductor of the orchestra called creation. Using a different image that is commonly used in the Hebrew Scriptures, we were created to care for and provide for creation the way a shepherd cares for his sheep.[7]

So, taking our cue from these two terms, what does it mean to be created in God's image? These two terms tell us we were created to use power the way God uses power. We were created to do what God did in creation. We were created to work in the face of chaos to bring forth that which is good. God created us to be God's partners in doing what God does—bringing out of chaos that which is good, light out of darkness, form out of formlessness, fullness out of emptiness, life out of nothingness. We were created to help create a world where each has a place. We were created to help fill the world with that which is good.

A Divine Spark

To be created in God's image, according to God's likeness means we carry a divine spark within us.

In creation, we were entrusted with creative powers that reflect God's creative power. We were entrusted with the ability to think and reason—our intellect—to guide how we use those creative powers. And we were entrusted with the ability to choose—our human free will. Our intellectual ability to think, evaluate, communicate, and negotiate becomes the basis of choosing how we use our creative powers. How we choose to use our creative powers determines whether we use them to contribute to the chaos or to call forth that which is good. In short, we were created for God's life.

Both male and female were created in God's image. Both possess creative powers and the ability to do what God did in the creation story.

The Babylonian creation story taught that we humans—and women, in particular—had to be feared and controlled because we were inherently violent. The biblical creation story teaches us just the opposite. It teaches us God created us in the divine likeness. In doing so, God trusted us, entrusting us with creative, intellectual abilities so that we can do what God did. In the face of chaos, we can use these abilities to call forth that which is good. In the face of that which is life-depleting, we can use these abilities to bring forth that which is life-giving.

How we view the other determines how we treat them. If we view them as different and as a threat, we will use our powers against them (as we will see in the story of Cain). In doing so, we contribute to the chaos in the world. If we view them as having been created in God's image, we will treat them with respect. We will seek to engage them as we seek to identify the path that leads to what is good.

We have been created in God's image. That truth shapes how we view others.

Dealing with Exile and Chaos

In addition to challenging the Babylonian understanding of humans, the biblical creation story also challenged the Hebrew people's understanding of their exile experience.

In their experience of exile in Babylon, the Hebrew people felt defeated, overwhelmed, and afraid. Having experienced devastating, life-altering loss, they believed God had abandoned them or, worse, that God was punishing them (Isaiah 40:27; 49:14). This creation narrative presented a whole different way of viewing the chaos they were experiencing. Rather than something to be feared as destructive, the narrative suggests that chaos was an opportunity for God to work. It was an opportunity for the Spirit to blow across the face of the chaos, bringing forth that which was good.

The narrative invites us to embrace a different way of viewing the chaos we experience in life. It calls us to view such times of chaos as opportunities for God to work. It also calls us to view such times as an opportunity for us to partner with God in that work. They are opportunities for us to use our abilities to think, to reason, and to choose. They are opportunities for us to be creative in how we exercise our power. They are opportunities for us to work with God in bringing forth that which is good.

We have been created in God's image. That truth shapes how we respond to the chaotic times of our lives.

Creating God in Our Image

While God has created us humans in God's image, we often repay the favor. We humans often create God in our image.

To create God in our image is to project onto God our thinking and our ways of functioning. We view God as relating to us the way we characteristically relate to one another.

We humans function out of merit-based thinking. We think in terms of deserving ... in terms of reward and punishment. Merit-based thinking naturally leads to us-them thinking in which we divide the world into those like us and those who are different. Us-them thinking fosters fear of those who are different. We view how they are different as a threat. Us-them thinking also leads to better than-less than thinking. We compare how we are different, invariably concluding "our way is best." We are right; they are wrong. Our ways are better than theirs. We are better than them.

When we create God in our image, we function as though God relates to us based on what we deserve, i.e., merit. Because deserving is a key word in our thinking and functioning, we seek to gain God's acceptance (love) by believing the right things and doing the right things. We act out of an underlying, often unrecognized fear. Our focus on believing the right things and doing the right things allows us to divide the world into us-them—those who have proper beliefs and behavior (those like us) and those who don't. We reward those who demonstrate proper belief and behavior with acceptance. We punish those who don't with judgment, rejection, and exclusion.

While we naturally think of God as being like us, the witness of scripture is clear: God is not like us. God's ways are not our ways.

> For my thoughts are not your thoughts,
> nor are your ways my ways, says the LORD.
> For as the heavens are higher than the earth,
> so are my ways higher than your ways and my thoughts
> than your thoughts (Isaiah 55:8—9).

Throughout scripture, the word *holy* is used to describe the LORD. The Hebrew word is an adjective that means different, other. To say the LORD is holy is to say the LORD is not like us. While we naturally relate out of merit-based thinking, God relates to us out grace and forgiveness. The psalmist clearly states "(the LORD) does not deal with us according to our sins, nor repay us according to our iniquities" (Psalm 103:10).

Merit-based language that emphasizes "the right way" to think and act and that creates us-them division is evidence that we have created God in our image.

A Guide for Personal Reflection and Journaling, for Group Conversation and Discussion

1. What is your "take away" from this chapter about being created in the image of God?
2. How might you be called to use your power in life-giving, life-enriching ways, working to bring good out of chaos?
3. Who is someone you struggle to honor as having been created "in the image of God?" What is the reason for that struggle?
4. What would it take to view an experience of chaos in your life as an opportunity for God to work?
5. In what ways have you created God in your own image?

CHAPTER 5

THE SEVENTH DAY

Thus the heavens and the earth were finished, and all their multitude. ²And on the seventh day God finished the work that he had done, and he rested on the seventh day from all the work that he had done. ³So God blessed the seventh day and hallowed it, because on it God rested from all the work that he had done in creation (Genesis 2:1-3).

What does it mean that God rested on the seventh day? And what significance does that have for us?

God's rest is tied to the completion of creation. "On the seventh day God finished the work that he had done, and he rested on the seventh day from all the work that he had done" (Genesis 2:2). God had finished the work of creating—bringing structure to that which was formless, filling that which was empty and void. Having declared creation "very good," God could rest, contented in what had been created.⁸ The Hebrew word translated as "rest" means "to stop, to cease." God stopped the work of creating because the work of creating was complete. God's rest is in relation to the work of creating the world.

God's rest does not mean God stopped working altogether. God continues to work. But God's work is a different kind of work from what God was doing in creating the world. God's work today is the work of bringing creation to maturity. God is at work bringing creation to the end for which it was created. God's work is bringing us humans to the end for which we were created—sharing God's life, being God's partner in doing God's work, using power in creative, life-giving ways, bringing that which is good out of the destructive forces of chaos. God's rest is God's work of bringing us to maturity.

The account of the seventh day does not include the phrase that brought every other day of creation to a close: "and there was evening and there was morning." The seventh day continues. God continues to work, bringing creation and us to maturity.[9]

God's rest on the seventh day included blessing and hallowing the seventh day.[10] "So God blessed the seventh day and hallowed it, because on it God rested from all the work that he had done in creation" (Genesis 2:3). The two terms mean the same thing. To bless is to make it holy.[11]

In the Decalogue (the Ten Commandments), the commandment to remember the Sabbath and keep it holy (Exodus 20:8—11) was tied to God's rest on the seventh day. The Hebrew adjective "holy" means "different" (as was noted above.) The seventh day was to be different from the other six days. It was to be set apart as a special day.

The Hebrew people saw the Sabbath as a gift. They viewed it as a blessing to be embraced with joy. What are the gifts that we receive when we make the seventh day different from the others?

Keeping the Sabbath reminds us of God's on-going work on the seventh day—the work of bringing us to spiritual maturity.

Keeping the Sabbath calls us to see beneath the surface of what is happening in our daily lives to the underlying process of growth into maturity. It teaches us to reflect on what our experience and on how we react to it. It teaches us to ask: where is God at work in this experience? What does God want to teach me through this experience? How does God want to mature me through this experience?

Keeping the Sabbath teaches us to trust God. It trains us to trust God's goodness and grace. It trains us to trust God's provision and abundance rather than depending solely upon our own abilities. It trains us to trust God's faithfulness to work in every aspect of life to bring us to maturity.

Keeping the Sabbath teaches us the holy rhythm of life. It teaches us there is a time to work and a time to rest, a time to put things in place and a time to trust the process to work, a time to design and create and a time to enjoy what is, a time to do and a time to be.

When we forget or neglect the seventh day, we miss the gifts the seventh day holds for us.

When we forget or neglect the seventh day, we forget what God wants to do in our lives. We forget God's commitment to bring us to maturity. We become blind to how God is at work, maturing us. In place of God's work, we fill our lives with things. We give our energies to acquiring and having. We fill our lives with activity. We forget how to be still and to simply be. We become anxious if we are not going and doing.

When we neglect the seventh day, we forget reflection. We fail to see beyond the surface. We neglect our spiritual growth. We become so busy going and doing, working and earning, acquiring and amassing that we miss how God is at work within our lives. We get trapped in looking for meaning somewhere else than in the life we have.

When we neglect the seventh day, we forget to trust. We forget God's goodness. We forget God's faithfulness. We work as though everything depends upon us and on what we can accomplish. We live as though there is never enough. We become consumed with having more—as though one more thing will fill the emptiness, as though one more activity will bring the fulfillment and joy for which we long.

When we forget the seventh day, we forget the holy rhythm of life. We make the seventh day like the other six. It becomes another day of doing, another day of work, another day of being busy. Our lives become full of demands and deadlines. Our lives become hurried and harried. Our spirits grow tired—a deep down soul tired. Who we are remains superficial and shallow, devoid of the depth and maturity God desires for us.

The seventh day is a gift—a part of the holy rhythm of life. It is a day set apart to teach us about God's desire for our maturity. It is a day set apart to teach us to see beneath the surface to how God is at work. It is a day to train us to trust God and God's faithfulness to us. It is a day to train us to keep in step with life's holy rhythm. It is a day set apart to teach us how to live.

A Guide for Personal Reflection and Journaling, for Group Conversation and Discussion

1. What is your "take away" from this chapter on the Sabbath day?
2. What gifts that the Sabbath day offers do you need to claim?
3. What does making the Sabbath day "holy" look like for you?

CHAPTER 6

MINING THE RICHES OF
THE CREATION STORY

The five narratives found in Genesis 1—11 are vehicles carrying the theological understanding of the ancient Hebrew people. This carefully crafted creation narrative proclaims ...

- God is the creator of the heavens and the earth. This reality inseparably ties creation to God and God to creation. Creation does not exist and cannot exist apart from God.
- The creation of the world was an intentional, decisive act of God. This intentionality suggests God has a purpose for creation.[12] God continues to be committed to and involved with creation as God seeks to bring that purpose into reality.
- God has authority over chaos and evil. Chaos and evil are a normal part of our life experience, but our experiences of chaos and evil are never the final word. God's authority over evil stirs hope in the face of discouragement and despair.
- God works in the midst of chaos, speaking into it to reverse its destructive, life-depleting nature, bringing forth life and that which is good.
- God uses power creatively, in life-giving, life-enriching ways. God never uses power to dominate or destroy. Rather, God uses power to bring forth that which is good.
- We humans are created in the image of God. We, like God, have creative powers that can be used to bring forth that which

is good. We were created to be God's partners in overcoming the chaos of life, bringing forth that which is good. We were created for God's kind of life and to do what God did in creating the world.

- Both male and female were created in the image of God. Both were created for God's kind of life. Both possess the power to be creative.
- God declared creation to be good, very good.
- God works to bring creation—particularly us humans!—to maturity.
- The seventh day of rest is a gift that teaches us and trains us in how to live life as God designed it.

A Guide for Personal Reflection and Journaling, for Group Conversation and Discussion

1. What is your "take away" from the study of the story of creation?
2. What does the story of creation tell you about God?
3. Having read this explanation of the creation story, how is your understanding of the story of creation different from before?

THE STORY OF THE GARDEN

Genesis 2:4—3:24

Genesis 2:4—3:24

T hese are the generations of the heavens and the earth when they were created.

In the day that the LORD God made the earth and the heavens, ⁵when no plant of the field was yet in the earth and no herb of the field had yet sprung up—for the LORD God had not caused it to rain upon the earth, and there was no one to till the ground; ⁶but a stream would rise from the earth, and water the whole face of the ground— ⁷then the LORD God formed man from the dust of the ground, and breathed into his nostrils the breath of life; and the man became a living being.

⁸And the LORD God planted a garden in Eden, in the east; and there he put the man whom he had formed. ⁹Out of the ground the LORD God made to grow every tree that is pleasant to the sight and good for food, the tree of life also in the midst of the garden, and the tree of the knowledge of good and evil. ¹⁰A river flows out of Eden to water the garden, and from there it divides and becomes four branches. ¹¹The name of the first is Pishon; it is the one that flows around the whole land of Havilah, where there is gold; ¹²and the gold of that land is good; bdellium and onyx stone are there. ¹³The name of the second river is Gihon; it is the one that flows around the whole land of Cush. ¹⁴The name of the third river is Tigris, which flows east of Assyria. And the fourth river is the Euphrates. ¹⁵The LORD God took the man and put him in the garden of Eden to till it and keep it.

¹⁶And the LORD God commanded the man, "You may freely eat of every tree of the garden; ¹⁷but of the tree of the knowledge of good and evil you shall not eat, for in the day that you eat of it you shall die."

¹⁸Then the LORD God said, "It is not good that the man should be alone; I will make him a helper as his partner." ¹⁹So out of the ground the LORD God formed every animal of the field and every bird of the air, and brought them to the man to see what he would call them; and whatever the man called every living creature, that was its name. ²⁰The man gave names to all cattle, and to the birds of the air, and to every animal of the field; but for the man there was not found a helper as his partner.

²¹So the LORD God caused a deep sleep to fall upon the man, and he slept; then he took one of his ribs and closed up its place with flesh. ²²And the rib that the LORD God had taken from the man he made into a woman and brought her to the man. ²³Then the man said, "This at

last is bone of my bones and flesh of my flesh; this one shall be called Woman, for out of Man this one was taken." ²⁴Therefore a man leaves his father and his mother and clings to his wife, and they become one flesh. ²⁵And the man and his wife were both naked, and were not ashamed.

Now the serpent was more crafty than any other wild animal that the LORD God had made. He said to the woman, "Did God say, 'You shall not eat from any tree in the garden'?" ²The woman said to the serpent, "We may eat of the fruit of the trees in the garden; ³but God said, 'You shall not eat of the fruit of the tree that is in the middle of the garden, nor shall you touch it, or you shall die.'" ⁴But the serpent said to the woman, "You will not die; ⁵for God knows that when you eat of it your eyes will be opened, and you will be like God, knowing good and evil."

⁶So when the woman saw that the tree was good for food, and that it was a delight to the eyes, and that the tree was to be desired to make one wise, she took of its fruit and ate; and she also gave some to her husband, who was with her, and he ate. ⁷Then the eyes of both were opened, and they knew that they were naked; and they sewed fig leaves together and made loincloths for themselves. ⁸They heard the sound of the LORD God walking in the garden at the time of the evening breeze, and the man and his wife hid themselves from the presence of the LORD God among the trees of the garden.

⁹But the LORD God called to the man, and said to him, "Where are you?" ¹⁰He said, "I heard the sound of you in the garden, and I was afraid, because I was naked; and I hid myself."

¹¹He said, "Who told you that you were naked? Have you eaten from the tree of which I commanded you not to eat?" ¹²The man said, "The woman whom you gave to be with me, she gave me fruit from the tree, and I ate." ¹³Then the LORD God said to the woman, "What is this that you have done?" The woman said, "The serpent tricked me, and I ate."

¹⁴The LORD God said to the serpent, "Because you have done this, cursed are you among all animals and among all wild creatures; upon your belly you shall go, and dust you shall eat all the days of your life. ¹⁵I will put enmity between you and the woman, and between your offspring and hers; he will strike your head, and you will strike his heel."

¹⁶To the woman he said, "I will greatly increase your pangs in childbearing; in pain you shall bring forth children, yet your desire shall be for your husband, and he shall rule over you."

¹⁷And to the man he said, "Because you have listened to the voice of your wife, and have eaten of the tree about which I commanded you, 'You shall not eat of it,' cursed is the ground because of you; in toil you shall eat of it all the days of your life; ¹⁸thorns and thistles it shall bring forth for you; and you shall eat the plants of the field. ¹⁹By the sweat of your face you shall eat bread until you return to the ground, for out of it you were taken; you are dust, and to dust you shall return."

²⁰The man named his wife Eve, because she was the mother of all living.

²¹And the Lord God made garments of skins for the man and for his wife, and clothed them.

²²Then the Lord God said, "See, the man has become like one of us, knowing good and evil; and now, he might reach out his hand and take also from the tree of life, and eat, and live forever"— ²³therefore the Lord God sent him forth from the garden of Eden, to till the ground from which he was taken. ²⁴He drove out the man; and at the east of the garden of Eden he placed the cherubim, and a sword flaming and turning to guard the way to the tree of life.

CHAPTER 7

INTRODUCING THE STORY OF THE GARDEN

When we move to the story of the garden, we move to a completely different kind of story than the story of creation in Genesis 1. The story of creation is a carefully designed creation narrative. It has a poetic flavor to it. Its design suggests the touch of a scholar. Its emphasis on the seventh day suggests an author associated with the priestly families. The story of the garden is the kind of story that was passed down orally from one generation to the next while sitting around a fire at night. It has an earthy nature rather than a poetic flavor. Its storyline shapes it rather than some carefully designed internal structure. It is much older than the story of creation. It is also from a different source. The story of creation comes from a priestly source. It spoke of God with the simple term God (*Elohim*). The story of the garden referred to God as "the LORD God" (Genesis 2:4b).

The story of the garden draws on earlier, royal court stories associated with the ancient Sumerian kingdoms which predated Assyria, Babylon, and Persia.

The story of the garden is not a creation narrative, per se, certainly not like the Genesis 1 story. It does relate God's creation of the man, of the garden, of the animals, and of the woman. But the creation portion of the story is developed to provide the backdrop for the main thrust of the story found in Genesis 3.

The story divides naturally into two sections, corresponding to the two chapters in Genesis that relate the story: Genesis 2:4—25, life in the garden; Genesis 3:1—24, loss of the garden.

The structure with the contrast between the two parts of the story points to the theological aspect of the story. The story addresses the question that all of us have asked at one time or another: "Why?" Why does life have to be so hard? Why does God allow suffering and pain and hardship? Why are human relationships so difficult? Why does God seem so distant?

Life in the garden, found in Genesis 2, reflects how we wish life could be—simple, full of pleasure and enjoyment, all our needs met, without problems to face or challenges to overcome, relationships that are meaningful and peaceful, untainted by fear—with God and one another. The loss of the garden, related in Genesis 3, provides an explanation of why life is what it is. It identifies the brokenness and alienation we experience in the relationships of our lives. The story reflects four primary relationships impacted by this brokenness and alienation: our relationship with God, our relationship with one another as men and women, our relationship with ourselves individually, and our relationship with creation. The story of the garden is a story about the relationships of our lives—what we wish they were, what they are, and why.

The story of the garden is introduced with the phrase "these are the generations of" (Genesis 2:4a). This phrase is the editor's note, indicating a shift of focus. It is used ten times in the book of Genesis.[13] Here, the editor's note is "these are the generations of the heavens and the earth when they were created." It is his way of saying "after the creation of the world, here's the next part of the story."

One challenge we face in reading the story of the garden lies in what we already believe it says. Without thinking, we inevitably read our understanding into the story. This inclination to "read into" blocks our ability to allow the story to be what it is and say what it says.

A common belief about this story is that it is the story of "The Fall." This understanding—influenced by John Milton's epic, seventeenth century poem Paradise Lost—views the story of the garden as the account of the first sin, leading to the expulsion from paradise. It understands the story as identifying the origin of sin. This understanding also views the serpent as Satan. Yet, the word "sin" is not used in the story nor is the serpent identified as Satan. None of the biblical writers ever refer to the Genesis 3 story in this way. The first time the serpent is identified as Satan is in the Jewish apocrypha written during the post-exilic period, after this story would have been written down and made a part of the Hebrew Scriptures. That association is reflected in Revelation 12:9 which speaks of "that ancient serpent, who is called the Devil and Satan, the deceiver of the whole world."

In his letter to the churches in Rome, the Apostle Paul drew on the story of Adam to draw a contrast between the first Adam and the second Adam—Christ Jesus. Adam's act of disobedience brought death; Christ Jesus's act of obedience brought life (Romans 5:12—21). But Paul's analogy and the thinking associated with The Fall are not the same.

A second challenge we face as we read the story of the garden is to "hear" it through the ears of the early audiences. What would the story have meant to the people of Israel during the experience of exile when the story became a part their collected scriptures? What would it have said to them? Viewing Genesis 3 as the story of The Fall bypasses the exiles and their experience of exile.

Is it possible for us to understand the story of the garden differently?

CHAPTER 8

THE STORY OF THE GARDEN, PART ONE: LIFE IN THE GARDEN, GENESIS 2:4–25

The first part of the garden story provides the backdrop to the second part. It sets the stage for what will come later in the story. This first part of the story divides into four sections, with each section relating God's creation of some part of creation:

> 2:4—7, the creation of the man, Adam
> 2:8—17, the creation of the garden for the man
> 2:18—20, the creation of the animals for the man
> 2:21—25, the creation of the woman for the man.

The Creation of the Man, Adam (Genesis 2:4—7)

The story begins with the LORD God's creation of the man, Adam. "Then the LORD God formed man from the dust of the ground, and breathed into his nostrils the breath of life; and the man became a living being" (Genesis 2:7). The earth was already in existence when God created the man. The man was the first thing God created to inhabit the earth.

Immediately, we are faced with an order of creation that is different from that found in the Genesis 1 creation narrative. In the story of creation, the man and woman were the last to be created. And man and woman were created together, in God's image. They were the apex of creation, the part that made everything God had made "very good." In the story of the garden, the man is created first. The woman is the last thing created.

Both accounts have the same emphasis: the special place we humans occupy in creation. The way each account communicated the truth is different, but the truth is the same. Our Western, scientifically-oriented thinking leads us to ask, "Which account is the right one, that is, the historically correct one?" The question overlooks the theological nature of these ancient texts, treating them as though they were historical records. Such disregard for the nature of the texts leads us away from the truth they present.

This truth—the special place we humans hold within creation—is expressed in two ways in this story. The man was the first thing God created. Everything else was created for the man's benefit—the garden, the animals, the woman. In addition, the man was created before there were plants or vegetation (Genesis 2:5). One of the two reasons given for this detail was the man was not yet available to till the land. The plants and vegetation needed the man's oversight and care.

The woman as the last thing the LORD God created includes her, along with the man, in this special place within creation. Her creation from the man's rib fulfilled his need for a companion and brought God's creating work to completion. She completed creation.

Two actions were involved in the creation of the man (Genesis 2:7). First, the LORD God fashioned the man's body from the dust of the ground. Then, the LORD God breathed into the man's nostrils the breath of life. This breath was what brought the man to life. These two actions reflect the dual nature of humanity. We are physical beings who are a part of the natural world. In addition, we are spiritual beings, the handiwork of God. Our life is tied to God just as it is tied to the physical realm. Our spiritual nature is also reflected in the fellowship the man and the woman enjoyed with the LORD God in the garden (Genesis 3).

The Creation of the Garden for the Man (Genesis 2:8—17)

Having created the man, the LORD God created a garden to be his home.

The garden was located "in Eden, in the east" (Genesis 2:8). The Hebrew word translated as "Eden" means delight. The name indicates the garden was a place of delight. The description of life in the garden leads us to think of Eden as paradise (again, reflecting the influence of Milton's Paradise Lost). Beyond this simple description, we do not know the physical location of the garden. While the location of the garden is a common question for Western, scientifically trained people, it was not a primary concern in the story. To pursue the question of the garden's location is to be diverted from what the story was designed to communicate.

Beyond its location in the east, the story relates four facts about the garden.

The story revolves around the trees of the garden. The garden was full of trees that were "pleasant to the sight and good for food" (Genesis 2:9). Thus, the garden was a place of beauty and abundance. It provided all the man's physical needs. Among the trees, two are specifically mentioned: the tree of life and the tree of the knowledge of good and evil. These two trees are singled out because of the central role they play in the second half of the story.

The garden was watered by a river that is not named. Outside the garden, the river divided into four tributaries which are named. Although they are named, these four rivers do not provide a clue to the garden's location. The first two bear the names of two of Ham's descendants as recorded in the genealogy of Noah found in Genesis 10. Genesis 10:6 identifies Cush as the son of Ham while Genesis 10:7 identifies Havilah as the son of Cush. The land of Cush is commonly understood as a reference to Ethiopia or Egypt. The river Gihon flowed around the land of Cush. Similarly, the Pishon is described as flowing around the land of Havilah. Havilah's association with Cush would lead us to associate this unknown land with Ethiopia or Africa, as well. In contrast to the uncertainty of the Gihon and Pishon, the Tigris and Euphrates were both known rivers. They provided the lifeblood for the lands of Assyria and Babylon. Thus, two of the named rivers are in the continent of Africa; two in the land of Assyria.

The man was placed in the garden "to till it and keep it" (Genesis 2:15). The man was entrusted with responsibility for the garden. He was to care for it and maintain it. This responsibility presents work as something that is good and healthy, a normal part of being human. The reciprocal nature of life is reflected in the man's role in the garden: the garden provided what the man needed physically; the man cared for, maintained, and worked the garden. Mutuality lies at the heart of life.

The key feature in the garden is the tree of the knowledge of good and evil and the command associated with it: "You may freely eat of every tree of the garden; but of the tree of the knowledge of good and evil you shall not eat, for in the day that you eat of it you shall die" (Genesis 2:16—17). The tree represents the central issue in the story: how to live in relationship with God. The LORD God created the man and then created the garden to provide for his needs. These acts of creation were gifts of grace. The expected response to such generosity is trust expressed in faithful obedience. Trust expressed in faithful obedience is the expression of a spirit of glad dependency.[14]

The LORD God's instruction regarding the tree begins with permission: "You may freely eat of every tree of the garden." The fruit of every tree in the garden was available to the man. He could choose freely from any of them. He had access to every tree with only one exception. The instruction begins with the gift of abundance. Trust, faithful obedience, and a spirit of glad dependency are grounded in the abundance of God's provision and generosity.

The only limitation placed on the man's choices was in relation to the tree of the knowledge of good and evil. This one tree was off limits. "Of the tree of the knowledge of good and evil you shall not eat." This limitation is explained by the phrase "for in the day that you eat of it you shall die." The prohibition was not arbitrary. It was not mean-spirited. It was intended to protect the man. It was rooted in care for the man and concern for his wellbeing.

Trust in God's provision and generosity is expressed in respecting the limits God has established. It is expressed in faithful obedience.

The Creation of the Animals for the Man (Genesis 2:18—20)

Like the garden, the animals were created for the man's benefit. Their creation was a part of and a prelude to the creation of the woman.

The account of the creation of the animals begins with the statement "It is not good that the man should be alone; I will make him a helper as his partner" (Genesis 2:18). Although the garden provided for all of the man's physical needs, something was still lacking. That lack was there even though the man enjoyed unhindered fellowship with the LORD God. This statement reflects our need for relationship with others. We are relational beings, created to live in relationship with others.

The animals were created and brought to the man. He named each of them as they were brought to him. Naming them suggests authority over them. They were not an equal. Naming may mean that the man was the one who named each species. He was the one who called a cow "cow." The text can also be understood as meaning the man gave each bird and animal a special name in the way we name our pets. This understanding reflects the relationship the man enjoyed with each bird and animal. Yet even with these many relationships, a suitable partner was not found for the man among the birds and animals. The man's need could not be met by anything in creation. He needed something more—an equal—one like himself. He needed someone who would be a companion.

All of the man's physical needs were met in the garden, but such was not enough. He was created for relationship. This detail in the story reminds us we cannot find fulfillment and meaning apart from meaningful relationships. Nothing else in creation can fill our need for relationship. We need one another.

The Creation of the Woman for the Man (Genesis 2:21—25)

The woman was created to address that which was lacking for the man in the garden. "It is not good that the man should be alone; I will make him a helper as his partner" (Genesis 2:18). The Hebrew phrase translated as "a helper as his partner" carries the idea of a helper who is like the man. Her creation out of the man's rib reinforces the idea as does the man's response to her, "This at last is bone of my bones and flesh of my flesh; this one shall be called Woman, for out of Man this one was taken" (Genesis 2:23). The woman was made of the same stuff as the man. Yet, she was different. She would complement him, not duplicate him. Thus, she could fill the man's need for a partner. As a helper and partner, the woman was created to share his role of tending and caring for the garden. In addition, she was created to share his life.

She was his companion. What was lacking in the garden for the man had been supplied. The man was no longer alone.

The woman's role as helper and partner implies an equal standing with the man. They were equals. She was in no way subordinate to the man. She stood alongside him as his equal.

The creation of the woman brought creation to fulfillment. The man now had a partner with whom to share the garden.

Part One of the garden story ends with two statements.

The first, in verse 24, identified this mutual partnership as the underlying pattern of marriage. "Therefore a man leaves his father and his mother and clings to his wife, and they become one flesh" (Genesis 2:24). This statement was likely inserted into the story by the editor as it does not develop the storyline. It reflects the Hebrew people's sacred view of marriage.

The second statement, in verse 25, described the relationship between the man and the woman. "And the man and his wife were both naked, and were not ashamed" (Genesis 2:25). The phrase "were not ashamed" implies their nakedness was more than physical nakedness. They were emotionally naked. They had nothing to hide from the other. They lived with openness and freedom in the relationship. This dimension of the relationship would be destroyed in Part Two of the story.

Part One ends with everything in place: the man and woman living together as partners in the garden. Their relationship was one of openness and freedom and (implied) willing cooperation. Their physical needs were met by the many trees of the garden. They enjoyed unfettered relationship with the LORD God. They enjoyed what we all long for: the harmony of paradise.

Everything that was put into place in Part One comes into play in Part Two of the story—the many trees of the garden, the tree of the knowledge of good and evil, the instructions and warning about the tree of knowledge, the animals (in the appearance of the serpent), the woman as the man's partner, their nakedness. The story can now move to the main part of the story in Part Two, Genesis 3.

CHAPTER 9

THE STORY OF THE GARDEN, PART TWO: LOSS OF THE GARDEN, GENESIS 3:1–24

Our challenge in dealing with Part Two is our familiarity with the story. Our knowledge of the story leads us to believe we know what it says and what it means. That assumption creates a barrier to hearing what the story says beyond what we already believe.

Like Part One of the garden story, Part Two falls into four segments:

> 3:1—7, the deception of the woman and man by the serpent
> 3:8—13, the confrontation of the man and woman by the LORD God
> 3:14—19, the consequences of the man and woman's choice
> 3:20—24, God's provision for and protection of the man and the woman.

The Deception of the Woman and Man by the Serpent, Genesis 3:1—7

With all the pieces in place (Part One), the story moves quickly to the central plot. The opening line carries as sense of foreboding as it introduces the serpent, describing it as "more crafty than any other wild animal that the LORD God had made" (Genesis 3:1).

The serpent is frequently identified as Satan, coming to tempt the man and woman into sin. The story itself does not identify the serpent as Satan. It merely describes the serpent as one of the wild creatures the LORD God had created.

Identifying the serpent as Satan is an example of how we read our understanding into the story. The understanding of Satan that we find in the New Testament did not develop until the post-Exilic period—just a few hundred years before the New Testament era and after this story would have been incorporated into the Hebrew Scriptures. It was not a part of the original telling of the story, either in its oral form or when it was first put into written form.

The character known as Satan appears only three times in the Hebrew Scriptures (Job 1:6—12, 2:1—7; 1 Chronicles 21:1; Zechariah 3:1—2). In each reference, the word used is a noun with the article "the"—the satan. It is not used as a personal name. The noun means "the adversary" or "the accuser." In each of these three references, the satan is presented as a member of God's heavenly court whose role was to bring accusations of wrongdoing against humans and to create challenges for them to overcome.

Interpreting the serpent as Satan gets us off on the wrong foot. It reads our New Testament understanding and theology back into the Old Testament story. In doing so, we unconsciously begin to hear the story the way we have always heard it, blocking our ability to hear it differently. In addition, interpreting the serpent as Satan literalizes the story, taking the focus off the meaning the story was designed to communicate. The challenge of interpretation is to allow the biblical text to say what it says—not what we think it says.

The serpent was one of the wild animals that the LORD God had created and brought to the man. Like all the other animals, it lived under the man and woman's authority and care. It had no power over the man or woman, no ability to force or coerce or control what they did. Its only power was the power of suggestion. That is the power it used.

The serpent is described as crafty, suggesting deceit and manipulation. The description alerts us: the serpent is up to no good. It is not to be trusted. The deceit is reflected in the serpent's approach of the woman. It began with a question in which it misquoted what the LORD God had said, "Did God say, 'You shall not eat from any tree in the garden'?" (Genesis 3:1b). The question was about God's instruction:

"What was it that God said was off limits?" The question reversed what the LORD God had actually said: "You may freely eat of every tree of the garden" (Genesis 2:16). In misquoting God, the serpent turned the woman's attention away from the abundance of the other trees to the tree of the knowledge of good and evil.

The woman was quick to correct the serpent's misunderstanding. She was the one who first spoke of the tree of knowledge of good and evil. "We may eat of the fruit of the trees in the garden; but God said, 'You shall not eat of the fruit of the tree that is in the middle of the garden, nor shall you touch it, or you shall die'" (Genesis 3:2—3). In quoting the LORD God's instructions, the woman added to what God had said—"nor shall you touch it." The serpent had the woman precisely where it wanted her. Now it could contradict what God had said. "But the serpent said to the woman, "You will not die; for God knows that when you eat of it your eyes will be opened, and you will be like God, knowing good and evil" (Genesis 3:4—5).

What the serpent told the woman was true, but not totally true. The serpent presented partial truth as though it were the full truth.

The seed was planted. The serpent's comment was designed to get the woman to question God, God's intentions, and God's trustworthiness. Its comment cast doubt on the LORD God and on the purpose of the instructions regarding the tree of the knowledge of good and evil. It introduced suspicion into the relationship with the LORD God. It hinted that God was withholding something from them, something that would vastly enrich their lives. It was designed to undermine the woman's complete trust in God and God's provision. And it worked. For the first time, the woman questioned what the LORD God had said.

The issue of faithful obedience is rooted in the question: "Can I really trust God?" It is a matter of who do I trust: God or myself? Do I trust what God says or my own wisdom?

The serpent's comment also played on the woman's desires—the desire for knowledge, the desire to be like God, the desire for more. The desire to move beyond the limitations of being human is one that is common to all of us. We are not like God. We are not all powerful nor are we omniscient. Not knowing or understanding is part of being human—one of the limitations. We want to move beyond this limitation. We want to know and understand. In our quest to know, we ask questions about what we don't understand. We ask "why?"

Knowing helps us overcome the challenges and move beyond the obstacles (limitations). It gives us a sense of control. It makes us feel powerful (omnipotent). Like the woman, we want more than what we have. This desire for more drives how we live. It dictates our lifestyles.

The desires that were stirred in the woman—the desire for knowledge, the desire to be like God, the desire for more—reflect the deep-seated fears with which we all live. We are afraid of being powerless and weak. When we are powerless and weak, we are incapable. We cannot measure up. To be incapable means we are inadequate. We are needy, dependent on others with little to offer. We are afraid of being powerless, weak, incapable, inadequate, needy, and dependent. In other words, we are afraid of the limitations that are a normal part of being human.

Our fears make us want to be like God! We want to be strong, knowing, self-sufficient, capable of taking care of ourselves, not needing anyone else—not even God!

"So when the woman saw that the tree was good for food, and that it was a delight to the eyes, and that the tree was to be desired to make one wise, she took of its fruit and ate; and she also gave some to her husband, who was with her, and he ate" (Genesis 3:6).

The words used to describe the other trees of the garden (Genesis 2:9) are used to describe the tree of knowledge: "pleasant to the sight and good for food." Like the other trees, this tree could meet the woman's physical needs and bring her pleasure. But this tree also addressed a desire the others did not. This tree offered them more. It offered the ability to know: "the tree was to be desired to make one wise." More than meeting physical needs and offering personal pleasure, this tree offered an intellectual component and stirred a spiritual desire.

With the rationale set in her mind, the woman made her decision and acted on it. She did what she had been instructed not to do. "She took of its fruit and ate; and she also gave some to her husband, who was with her, and he ate" (Genesis 3:6b). The man chose along with her, joining her in eating the fruit of the tree. The LORD God had created the woman to be the man's companion and partner. They were companions and partners in this decision and the actions it produced.

Their actions seem simple enough, almost innocent, but they reflect something profound: the choice to trust their own wisdom over God's, the choice to follow their own will rather than God's instructions, the choice to live in self-reliance rather than in trusting, faithful obedience.

Their choice—an exercise of the will—had immediate, major consequences.

What the serpent said was indeed true. The man and the woman did not die immediately. But what the LORD God said was also true. Death now became a part of their reality (as we shall see at the end of the story, Genesis 3:22—24). And, as the serpent said, their eyes were opened so that they knew good and evil like God. But they did not become like God as the serpent said they would. Instead, the knowledge they gained brought self-awareness and, with it, shame and fear. "Then the eyes of both were opened, and they knew that they were naked; and they sewed fig leaves together and made loincloths for themselves" (Genesis 3:7).

The first impact of their decision was on their relationship with one another. Genesis 2:25 described their relationship as "naked, and were not ashamed." Their relationship was one of openness and freedom with nothing to hide. Their decision to eat of the fruit of the tree of knowledge destroyed that dynamic. They immediately recognized their nakedness. Being known was no longer comfortable. It was frightening, embarrassing. They felt exposed. Immediately, they tried to hide their nakedness by sewing fig leaves together to use as loincloths.

Hiding behind fig leaves is a normal dynamic in human relationships. We fear being known, afraid of being judged and rejected. Although we were created for relationships in which we know and are known, we settle for superficial relationships. We keep others at an arm's length, afraid of letting them get too close to us.

Our fear of being known is tied to shame. Genesis 2:25 specifically stated the man and woman "were not ashamed" of their nakedness. But now, a sense of shame is an inherent part of our human condition and a determining factor in how we relate to one another. It robs us of the freedom to be open with one another. It is a barrier to deep, meaningful relationships in which we know and are known.

Our shame arises out of our awareness that we have failed to live up to the expectations of others and society—and God! We know we have broken the rules. In spite of what we were taught was right, we have chosen to follow our own will and go our own way—just as the man and the woman did in the story of the garden.[15]

The story clearly states the man and the woman sought to hide their nakedness by sewing loin cloths. That fact hints at the discomfort (shame?) we have with sexuality, represented in our loins (genitals). It seems we do not know how to deal with human sexuality in a healthy, open way. Many Western cultures, following Victorian and Puritan values, tell us to cover it up (with fig leaves?!). Yet, the more we attempt to keep it hidden out of sight, the more we seem to flaunt it. Consider how our fashions are based upon revealing or hiding the human body or how many of our forms of entertainment incorporate sexual innuendo and/or explicit sexual content or how sex is used to sell products. Our inability to deal openly with human sexuality gives it a mysterious power. We become obsessed with it, both as individuals and as a society. Sadly, religion has often led the effort to hide sexuality behind some kind of fig leaves.

The story of the garden tells us the way we deal with our sense of shame is by hiding behind fig leaves. Our hiding involves more than not allowing others to know us other than superficially. It also involves hiding from ourselves (as the story of the garden will reflect as it unfolds). We often go to great lengths to avoid the pain of our shame.

The reference to fig leaves would have brought a chuckle from those who first heard the story. Fig leaves are rough and scratchy. The man and the woman used scratchy materials to sew coverings for the most sensitive parts of their body.

The Confrontation of the Man and Woman by the LORD God, Genesis 3:8—13

The introduction of shame into their relationship, resulting in the loss of openness and freedom with one another, was just the first consequence of the man and woman's action. This next part of the story portrays two additional consequences: the loss of freedom in their relationship with God and the inability to deal honestly with themselves. Hiding was the means by which the two sought to deal with these consequences.

"They heard the sound of the LORD God walking in the garden at the time of the evening breeze" (Genesis 3:8). This simple statement reflects the fellowship the couple enjoyed with the LORD God. They regularly spent time together at the end of the day. As was their pattern, the LORD God came to visit with them. But the special fellowship that was the background to this statement is overshadowed with foreboding. They heard the LORD God coming. The sound of the LORD God's approach stirred fear within them. In this statement, we can hear the echo of something most children have said at one time or another, "Quick! Hide! Someone's coming!"

The couple's reaction was to hide. They sought to avoid facing the One whose instructions they had ignored and violated. Their hiding is an accurate reflection of how we deal with our failures and wrongdoing. We attempt to hide them from others, particularly from those in positions of power and authority. We attempt to cover up what we have done. Dishonesty and cover up became the pattern of their relationship with the LORD God.

Their hiding points to the second consequence of their choice: a loss of freedom in their relationship with the LORD God. The freedom and joy they once enjoyed were replaced with hiding and avoiding. Undoubtedly, most of us can identify with what the couple felt and did. Fearing God's reaction to our wrongdoing, we too attempt to hide from God and avoid having to face God. Such is a part of our human condition.

But God cannot be avoided.

As the couple hid, the LORD God began searching for them, calling out to the man: "Where are you?" (Genesis 3:9). This one line of the story embodies the story of all of scripture: God searching for us, calling out to us, reaching out to us as we hide and run from God.

Unable to avoid the inevitable encounter with the LORD God, the man hesitantly called back from behind the bushes in which he hid: "I heard the sound of you in the garden, and I was afraid" (Genesis 3:10). Fear, not freedom, was now the dominant tone of the man's relationship with the LORD God. And the reason for the fear: "because I was naked." And what he did because of his fear: "and I hid myself." Like the man, afraid of being found out—naked, exposed—we hide.

There were only two explanations for how the man knew he was naked: someone told him or he ate the fruit of the tree that he had been commanded not to eat. The LORD God presented the two options and asked for an explanation (Genesis 3:11).

Who of us has not done what the man did? Being honest, acknowledging the truth was too painful and too frightening. So the man deflected the LORD God's focus by blaming the woman.

He shifted the focus from himself to her. He sought to avoid any responsibility for the situation by placing the responsibility on her. "The woman whom you gave to be with me, she gave me fruit from the tree, and I ate" (Genesis 3:12) Yes, he ate the fruit but only because of what she did. It was her fault. Not only did the man blame the woman, he also blamed God: "whom you gave to be with me."

The LORD God continued to probe, turning to the woman. The LORD God's question of the woman echoes through the chambers of our childhood memories, "What did you do?"

The woman's response mirrored the man's. She admitted she ate the fruit from the tree but blamed the serpent for tricking her into doing so. It was the serpent's fault. She was not responsible.

The man and the woman's response to the LORD God reveal a third consequence of their choice: the inability to be honest with oneself and, consequently, with God. This inability was expressed in blaming.

The Consequences of the Man and Woman's Choice, Genesis 3:14—19

Choices have consequences.

The LORD God created the man and the woman with the ability to choose—what is commonly called free will. The tree of the knowledge of good and evil, along with the instructions regarding it, reflect this divine gift. Free will means having the power to choose. In this situation, the couple could choose to follow the LORD God's directive-instruction or to disregard and violate it. But free will also means we get what we choose. Having given the man and woman the gift of choice, the LORD God respected their choice by giving them what they choose.

The serpent had told the woman that eating of the tree of the knowledge of good and evil would make her life better. Her eyes would be opened. She would know good and evil. She would be like God. What the serpent didn't tell her was what else eating of the tree would bring. It was left to the LORD God to tell her, along with the man, that news.

The story has already related several consequences of the couple's choice. They became aware of their nakedness, stirring shame and fear. The freedom and openness they enjoyed with one another was replaced with fear that caused them to hide from one another behind fig leaves. Their companionship was fractured with blaming. The freedom and openness they enjoyed with the LORD God was replaced with shame and fear that caused them to hide from the LORD God and avoid the Divine Presence. The shame and fear they felt led them to deflect personal responsibility by blaming. Their blaming posture reflected an inner brokenness. But the impact of the couple's choice went beyond these the story has already portrayed. And it extended beyond just the two of them.

The serpent was held accountable for its role in the couple's choice. The LORD God addressed it first:

> Because you have done this, cursed are you among all animals and among all wild creatures; upon your belly you shall go, and dust you shall eat all the days of your life. I will put enmity between you and the woman, and between your offspring and hers; he will strike your head, and you will strike his heel" (Genesis 3:14—15).

The consequence for the serpent was expressed as a curse. It lost its standing among the creatures God had created. It was relegated to crawling on the ground, eating dust. It would be feared by the woman and her offspring, creating animosity and enmity between them. Humans would seek to kill it—strike your head—while it would seek to kill them—strike his heel.[16]

The woman would experience two additional consequences in addition to what she had already experienced (Genesis 3:16). The first consequence had to do with her unique ability to bear children. That process would be filled with pain.[17] In spite of that pain, the woman would still desire her husband sexually. Another way of understanding the phrase "your desire shall be for your husband" is as a reference to the woman's sense of dependence upon her husband. In addition, her relationship with her husband would be different in one significant way: "he shall rule over you." The equality and mutuality the man and woman enjoyed when she was created to be a helper and companion— like him, but different, a compliment to him, not a duplication of him—was replaced by male domination. Male domination or patriarchy is here presented as part of the brokenness of creation, not as a part of God's original design.

Jesus rejected male domination. He related to women out of God's original design, treating them with dignity and respect as equal members of the covenant community. He included them in his circle of disciples (see Luke 8:1—3). The Apostle Paul followed Jesus's lead, writing to the Galatian churches, "in Christ Jesus you are all children of God through faith. There is no longer Jew or Greek, there is no longer slave or free, there is no longer male or female; for all of you are one in Christ Jesus" (Galatians 3:26, 28). In Christ and in Christian communities, the social distinctions reflecting the brokenness of human relationships are set aside, replaced by oneness in Christ.[18]

The additional consequences for the man were in relation to his role in tending the garden (Genesis 2:15). Just as the woman's childbearing role was negatively impacted, so was the man's work. Just as the woman's childbearing role would be filled with pain, the man's work would be filled with hard work—toil—requiring great exertions of energy—sweat. The land itself, once the source of his provision and delight, would now present challenges. He would have to contend with weeds such as thorns and thistles. The ground, once his ally in productivity, would now seem to be more of an adversary.

The ground is said to have been cursed because of the couple's choice. Creation itself was impacted.[19] Creation is the fourth relationship impacted by the couple's disobedience.

While the serpent and the ground were said to be cursed, the term was not applied to either the woman or the man.

The LORD God's command to not eat of the tree of knowledge of good and evil included the warning "for in the day that you eat of it you shall die" (Genesis 2:17). The serpent dismissed the warning, telling the woman "you will not die" (Genesis 3:4). Now the truth of the LORD God's warning became evident. Death is the final theme of the man's consequences: "until you return to the ground, for out of it you were taken; you are dust, and to dust you shall return" (Genesis 3:19).

Some refer to these verses as God's judgment on the couple for their act of disobedience. A better way of describing them is to speak of consequences. God had warned them of the consequences (impact). Once they made the choice, God gave them what they chose. Perhaps what we call judgment is nothing more than living with the consequences of our choices. It is certainly not an expression of any anger on God's part.[20]

God's Provision and Protection of the Man and the Woman, Genesis 3:20—24

The consequences were severe. Brokenness shattered the wholeness described in Part One of the story. Shame replaced openness. Fear replaced freedom. Hiding and blaming replaced the joy of life shared in relationship. Male domination replaced the mutuality of partnership and the equality of companions who complimented one another. Toil and struggle replaced the tilling and caring of the garden. Thorns and thistles replaced the abundance of fruit from the trees of the garden. The prospect of death invaded their awareness. Fear of God replaced the fellowship the couple once enjoyed with the LORD God in the cool of the day.

But the consequences are not the end of the story. Judgment is never the last word in the Hebrew Scriptures. The LORD never abandons or gives up on the people (or us!).[21] In the last segment of the story, the LORD God responded to the need of the couple as they lived in their new reality. The LORD God's actions were expressions of compassion and care.[22] Were we to use New Testament language, we would say they were expressions of grace.

The first act in this part of the story is done by the man. "The man named his wife Eve, because she was the mother of all living" (Genesis 3:20). The naming brings to mind the man's naming of the animals in Part One of the garden story (Genesis 2:19). There, the naming reflected the man's authority over the animals. Here, the naming of the woman can be seen as an expression of the new dynamic in the relationship in which the man now ruled over the woman (Genesis 3:16c). Another way of understanding this verse is to focus on the name Eve rather than on the act of naming. The name Eve is given because the woman is "the mother of all living." Given the prospect of death, the woman becomes the means by which life continues. This understanding makes the verse an expression of hope in the face of death. In spite of the reality of death, life continues through the role of the woman. In addition, her name gives her a new way of being known. Rather than being known as the means by which death entered the world (through her decision to eat of the fruit of the tree of the knowledge of good and evil), she would be known as the source of life.

The issue of nakedness and all it implies runs throughout the story of the garden. It became the first thing the couple realized after they ate of the fruit of the tree of the knowledge of good and evil. It became the source of their shame and fear. They feebly attempted to deal with it by sewing fig leaves together for loin cloths. The LORD God's first act in this part of the story was to address this source of their shame and fear. "And the LORD God made garments of skins for the man and for his wife, and clothed them" (Genesis 3:21). The LORD God clothed them with garments made of animal skins. This act assumes an animal was killed so the man's nakedness could be covered. The death would have come at the hand of the LORD God. This act carries overtones of the Hebrew sacrificial system in which animals were offered to atone (cover) sin.

The Lord God's second act in this part of the story can be understood as an act of judgment but it is explained as an act of compassion. The LORD God sent or drove the man (and the woman although she is not specifically mentioned) from the garden. The term drove is stronger than the term sent. It implies force used.[23]

The expulsion from the garden is described as a protective measure. The garden had yet another tree that played a vital role for the couple in the garden. It was the tree of life. Its name suggests this tree was the means by which the couple could avoid the reality of death. But living forever would condemn them to living forever with the pain and brokenness of their new reality. The LORD God acted to protect them from such a fate, even though it meant allowing them to experience the reality of death. An angel was posted to protect the tree of life, denying the couple access to it.

The expulsion from the garden was yet another consequence of the couple's act of disobedience.

A Guide for Personal Reflection and Journaling, for Group Conversation and Discussion

1. What new thought or understanding did you experience about the story of the garden?
2. How does that new thought or understanding impact the way you read the story?
3. With what part(s) of the story do you identify?

CHAPTER 10

MINING THE RICHES OF THE
STORY OF THE GARDEN

The story of the garden mirrors our experiences in life. Therein is its power. It holds up for us a mirror in which we can see ourselves—our proclivity to trust our own thinking and follow our own way rather than do what we are told (the distrust of authority), the fear that permeates our relationships, the fig leaves behind which we hide, the shame that we attempt to hide, our inclination to blame others as a way to avoid personal responsibility, our struggles and toil along with the thorns and thistles with which we contend, our fear of death. It also reflects our longings and desires—for life to be simple and less painful, for a sense of abundance to offset our fear of scarcity, for relationships that are not so complicated, for a way to avoid the reality of death and the pain it brings. The story is the story of our human condition and all that it entails.

The story is not a theological statement like the story of creation in Genesis 1. The ancient Hebrew storytellers were not attempting to teach theology or refute another theology (as with the Genesis 1 creation story). Instead, they described what life is like. The story is a description of our human condition. The only part of the story that might be described as a theological statement is the verse at the end of Part One about marriage: "therefore a man leaves his father and his mother and clings to his wife, and they become one flesh" (Genesis 2:24). That verse was probably not a part of the original story. It was inserted somewhere along the way.

And yet the story is full of theology. Because it speaks to our life experience and describes our human condition, it raises theological issues. The story does not state the issues or develop them. It merely stirs them in our minds. Because the story mirrors our human condition, it touches some of life's most perplexing issues and theological questions:

> What is our nature as human beings?
> What is our relationship as human beings with the rest of creation?
> What is the nature of the relationship between men and women?
> What is the nature of our relationship with God?
> What is the relationship between human free will and divine sovereignty?
> Where is the source of evil and suffering? How are we to understand them?
> What is sin? What are its consequences?

What follows is my attempt to speak to some of the theological issues the garden story raises.

The Tree of the Knowledge of Good and Evil: Human Free Will and the Sovereignty of God

The tree of the knowledge of good and evil is an indispensable component in the story of the garden. Everything that happens revolves around this tree and the instructions that go with it. Without this tree, there is no story.

The tree and the LORD God's instructions-prohibition regarding it raise the issue of human free will. The instructions-prohibition assumes the power to choose. The LORD God created the couple (and us) with the ability and responsibility to choose. This God-given ability gives us the power to be partial architects of our own lives. Our choices allow us to shape our lives—as Part Two of the story demonstrated. This ability is part of what distinguishes us from all other living creatures.

Free will is only possible because God respects our choices, giving us what we choose. Thus, the ability and responsibility to choose includes getting what we choose. Our choices have consequences. What and how we choose determines what the consequences are. The consequence for eating of the forbidden fruit was clearly stated: "you shall surely die" (Genesis 2:17). Death was more than physical death. As the story unfolded, we saw that death meant separation and alienation in our relationships. The consequence of the man and woman's choice to not trust God was alienation. Alienation became the norm of the man and woman's relationship with God, with one another, with creation, and even within their own selves.

Human free will raises the issue of God's sovereignty. How do we reconcile the concept of human free will with God's sovereignty?

Most efforts approach the dilemma as an either-or proposition.[24] One position takes priority over the other, basically nullifying the other. In this approach, God's sovereignty is generally the default position. After all, God is God! Sovereignty means God is all powerful and, thus, in control of everything. The implication is nothing happens apart from God's will. This understanding is reflected in such comments as "it's God's will" and "God has a purpose." This position views God's sovereignty as greater than human free will. God's sovereignty trumps human free will.

The other position—advocating human free will—challenges this way of thinking. Free will means our choices, not God, cause some things to happen. God does not overrule our choices or the consequences of those choices.

Our Western, scientifically-oriented thinking treats these two issues as mutually exclusive. You can have one but not the other. In our thinking, the two issues represent two opposite poles on a spectrum. We feel compelled to choose one over the other.

The struggle with evil and suffering becomes an issue when divine sovereignty takes priority over human free will. We inevitably ask the question "why?" If God is sovereign, i.e., all powerful, why does God allow evil and suffering? This struggle is commonly expressed in the false dichotomy: if God is all powerful, then God cannot be all loving. If God is all loving, then God cannot be all powerful.

The story of the garden does not engage in this kind of either-or thinking. It does not ask us to choose one position over the other. The story presents both views. The LORD God is sovereign *and* the man had the freedom to choose.

Hebrew scholars avoid this false dichotomy by speaking of divine self-limitation. They use the Hebrew word for a raisin to describe God's action. Like a raison, God shriveled up. In order to respect the man's choice, God did not exercise the sovereignty that is a part of being God. God chose to limit how divine sovereignty was used. God chose to live out of self-limitation.

Divine self-limitation acknowledges that God has the ability to force a choice (God's sovereignty), but understands God will not do so. God respects the choices we make (free will), even when the choice and its consequence are devastating and destructive.

Divine self-limitation does not mean God abandons sovereignty. God's sovereignty is exercised by working in the midst of human choices and their consequences to bring forth that which is good. This understanding is reflected in the story of creation in Genesis 1. In it, God worked in the midst of chaos to bring forth that which was good. As we will saw in Part Two of the garden story, God did not abandon the man and woman. Rather, God continued to work, responding with compassion, relating out of grace.

This understanding is reflected in the nation's experience of exile in Babylon. They interpreted their experience of exile as the consequences of their failure to live in faithful obedience. Yet the unidentified prophet to the exiles (Isaiah 40—55) understood that the LORD had not abandoned them. The LORD was at work redeeming them from their "death" experience (Isaiah 42:1—9; 42:18—43:7; 43:16—21).

The Apostle Paul spoke of God's work in all things in his letter to the churches of Rome. He also identified the end for which God works:

> And we know that in all things God works for the good of those who love him, who have been called according to his purpose. For those God foreknew he also predestined to be conformed to the image of his Son, that he might be the firstborn among many brothers and sisters (Romans 8:28-29 NIV).[25]

God's sovereignty is exercised by working in the midst of what happens (just as God moved across the face of chaos in the creation story, working to bring order to that which was formless and to fill that which was empty). God works to transform the experience "for good."

That good is identified in verse 29 as conforming us to the image of the Son. God works in all of life's experiences to help us grow spiritually. God works in all things to bring us to Christ-like spiritual maturity.[26]

The Trees of the Garden and God's Will

Closely related to the issues of free will and divine sovereignty is the concept of God's will.

Many speak of finding and doing God's will. The common understanding is God's will is one thing—the right choice, the right job, the right person to marry, the right path. Beneath this quest for God's will is the assumption that finding and doing God's will somehow guarantee success or happiness. By finding and doing God's will, we are protected from failure and life's pain.

The prohibition about the tree of knowledge suggests a different way of understanding this issue of God's will. The man was given permission to eat of any of the many trees in the garden. Only one was forbidden. The implication is the only way for the man "to be outside God's will" was to eat of the one tree that had been prohibited. Eating of any other tree would have been "within God's will."

God did not give us the ability to choose (free will) with the intent to limit our choices to one "right" thing. God gave us the ability to choose so we could choose from many options. The only way "to be outside of God's will" is to disobey what God has expressly forbidden.

The story of the garden does not expressly deal with the issues of God's sovereignty, human free will, or God's will. The story simply tells a story. But the story raises these theological issues in our minds. They are a natural outgrowth of hearing the story. These theological concepts are embedded in the tree of the knowledge of good and evil with its instruction-prohibition.

For in the Day You Eat of It: Consequences, not Judgment

The LORD God's instructions regarding the tree of knowledge of good and evil included a warning: "for in the day you eat of it you shall die" (Genesis 2:17). The prohibition was not arbitrary. It was given out of concern. It was an attempt to protect. "This is what will happen if you do." The warning communicated a reality of life: choices have consequences. The consequences of the couple's choice are clearly reflected in the story (as detailed above).

We humans are prone to speak of judgment rather than consequences. We commonly think in terms of punishment. This inclination is rooted in merit-based thinking which uses the language of earning and deserving. Merit-based, earning-deserving thinking governs how we humans live in relationship. How we view and treat the other is based upon what we believe they deserve.

While merit-based thinking and relating is engrained in our human condition, it is not God's way. God relates out of grace. God relates to us out of who God is, not in reaction to what we do or what we deserve. The psalmist clearly stated this reality:

> (The LORD) does not deal with us according to our sins,
> nor repay us according to our iniquities.
> For as the heavens are high above the earth,
> so great is his steadfast love toward those who fear him;
> as far as the east is from the west,
> so far he removes our transgressions from us.
> as a father has compassion for his children,
> so the LORD has compassion for those who fear him.
> For he knows how we were made;
> he remembers that we are dust (Psalm 103:10—14).

God always responds to us out of and in harmony with the Divine Nature. God's steadfast, faithful love means God never abandons us or gives up on us. God responds to us with compassion and mercy. God responds to our transgressions and sins with forgiveness.[27]

God's forgiveness does not free us from the consequences of our choices.[28] Human free will requires that we get what we choose, even when what we choose is harmful and destructive. Consequences are not God punishing us for what we chose (our concept of judgment). Rather, consequences are God giving us what we chose.

This understanding is reflected in the Apostle Paul's teaching about the wrath of God in Romans 1:18—32. Paul did not speak of wrath as anger or punishment. Rather, he spoke of wrath as a divine principle written into the fabric of life. That principle is "choices have consequences." Choices are like seeds which are planted. They sprout and produce fruit. God's wrath is God allowing us to experience the consequences of what we choose. Three times in the text, Paul used the phrase "God gave them over" (Romans 1:24, 26, 28). God gave them the natural results of what they chose. Each successive statement of "God gave them over" describes a more perverse result. The perversion grew the more the people continued to choose it. The choice is like a mutating flu virus. Each mutation becomes worse than the one before it.

Experiencing the negative consequences of our choices is not God punishing us for those choices. It is simply God giving us what we chose. The consequences of sin are its own punishment (as we saw in the story of the garden).

The last part of the story proclaims another truth: God does not abandon us to our consequences. Even as we deal with what we chose, God continues to be faithful to us. God continues to respond to us with compassion. God continues to address our needs.

Exodus 34:7b states that the impact of our sin (the consequences of our choices) extends to the third and fourth generation. Our choices impact our grandchildren and great-grandchildren. Exodus 34:6 states that God's steadfast, faithful love extends to the thousandth generation. The contrast of the third and fourth generation with the thousandth generation teaches God's faithful love is greater than the consequences of our choices.

The Serpent: the Problem of Evil and Its Source

The serpent and its deception raises the issue of evil—that which goes against God and the ways of God. What is the source of evil? From where does it come?

A common way of addressing this issue is by using dualistic thinking. Dualistic thinking is either-or thinking that, as we saw above, sets two seemingly opposite positions in opposition to one another. In this approach, good is set over against evil; God is set over against an evil being (often identified as Satan or the devil). The Hebrew people did not engage in this kind of dualistic approach to the problem of evil.[29] We violate the story when we read such thinking back into the story by identifying the serpent as Satan.

Throughout scripture, evil is viewed as a part of life. It exists under the authority of God. In the story of the garden, the serpent who enticed the woman to trust her own thinking rather than follow God's instructions was one of the creatures God had created. It was a part of creation. It did not stand outside of creation as an independent power opposing God.

This view of evil, existing under the authority of God, is consistent throughout the scriptural witness. In doing so, the scriptures leave the issue of evil in the realm of mystery, beyond human understanding.

Attempting to resolve the mystery with dualistic thinking—pitting God against an evil being (Satan, the devil, Beelzebul)—naturally leads to thinking in terms of conflict and conquest. One must win; the other must lose and be destroyed. This approach ignores the nature of God and overlooks how God uses power. As the Genesis 1 creation story reflects, God does not use power to destroy. Rather, God works in the midst of chaos and that which we call evil to bring forth that which is good. God "defeats" evil by transforming it and its impact.

The understanding of Satan that is reflected in New Testament writings developed during the post-exilic period under the influence of Persian religious thought, specifically Zoroastrianism. Zoroastrianism was thoroughly dualistic. This Persian influence can be seen in the Jewish writings of the post-exilic period called the Apocrypha. In those writings, Satan is identified as the means by which death entered the world (The Wisdom of Solomon 2:24). Satan is first associated with Eve in those writing.

The understanding of Satan found in the New Testament writings does not portray Satan as an evil being on the same level as God. Satan is viewed as one of the angels of God and, thus, part of God's creation. Satan lives under the authority of God and with the permission of God. He has rebelled against the authority of God (see Revelation 12:3—4, 7—9 and Luke 10:18) but he does not have God's kind of power (sovereignty). His power is limited. His primary power, as we saw in the story, is the power of suggestion.

Evil, like human free will, exists alongside the sovereignty of God. Its origin and its resolution lie in the realm of mystery.

You Will Be Like God: the Struggle with Being Human

The serpent's promise "you will be like God" hits a nerve for many, if not most, of us. We don't like being human.

Being human means living with limitations. We do not have unlimited strength or energy or knowledge or ability. We don't have unlimited anything. Sometimes we run out of what we do have. During those times, we don't have enough of what is needed. We run short of energy, patience, understanding, knowledge, love, etc. We struggle with limited financial resources. When we run out of what we have, we are unable to deal with our situation as we would like. We are confronted with being inadequate.

Our limitations translate into needs. We have to replenish our depleted supply. We need to refill our tanks. We have to refuel. We have to do those things that restore what has been used up—rest, eat, sleep, play, learn. Our limitations and needs can leave us feeling weak and vulnerable. They make us dependent.

Being human also means we are not yet full grown. We are still in process. That means we don't always measure up.

We don't like being human. We don't like being limited, powerless, needy, inadequate, or dependent. When we feel limited or powerless or needy or inadequate or dependent, we feel no good. We believe no one will want us or value us. We fear being left out and abandoned. We are afraid of being hurt. No wonder we want to escape our humanness!

No, we don't like being human. We want to be powerful, capable, more than adequate, independent, self-sufficient. We want to be like God.

Interestingly, the serpent's promise that we can be like God is true … just not in the way the serpent meant it. We will never escape our humanness with its limitations, needs, dependency, and in-process nature. But we can become like God.

The essence of the spiritual journey is growing into Christ-like maturity. It is a journey of personal transformation and growth in which the character of God is engrained within. Having been created in the likeness of God (Genesis 1:26), we are now being recreated in the likeness of Christ. As we saw in the discussion of the seventh day in the story of creation, God is at work to bring us to maturity, a maturity that reflects God's own nature.

This profound truth is expressed throughout scripture. The prophet Jeremiah spoke of God's law being written on our hearts (Jeremiah 31:33), an image that speaks of inner transformation. The Apostle Paul spoke of being conformed to the image of the Son (Romans 8:29). In his letter to the Corinthians, he spoke of the Spirit's work of transforming us into the image of Christ "from one degree of glory to another" (2 Corinthians 3:18) and of our inner nature being renewed (2 Corinthians 4:16). The writer of Ephesians spoke of growing up into "maturity, to the measure of the full stature of Christ" (Ephesians 4:13) and of putting on "the new self, created according to the likeness of God in true righteousness and holiness" (Ephesians 4:24). Being like God, possessing God's nature as our own, is the intended end of the spiritual journey.

The serpent lied to the woman, but in the lie, it proclaimed a truth. The Spirit is recreating us in the likeness of God. Before God is through with us, we will possess God's nature as our own, empowering us to love as Jesus loved and to love those Jesus loved. The Spirit is God's guarantee of this reality (Ephesians 1:13—14). The term the biblical writer used in this text from Ephesians is a financial term meaning down payment or earnest money. The Spirit is God's down payment guaranteeing the fulfillment of the contract. The Spirit will continue to work in our hearts and minds until we are fully conformed into the likeness of Christ.

You Will Not Die: Submitting to and Rebelling Against Authority

The serpent led the woman to disobey God's command by casting doubt on God's intent. Its words created suspicion of God and of the stated reason behind the command to not eat of the fruit of the tree of knowledge of good and evil. It raised the issue of trust. It stirred trust-oriented questions: are you going to trust what the LORD God said or your own wisdom? Are you going to do what someone else says or follow your own way?

Underlying the serpent's tactic with the woman is the issue of how we view and relate to authority. Do we trust someone over us to have our best interest in mind?

How we deal with the issue of authority is shaped by our basic personality as well as by our experience of authority in our formative years. Some of us readily conform to rules and laws as the path to being safe and secure. We are inclined to comply with those who hold positions of authority. Others of us by nature are more skeptical and distrustful of those in positions of authority, leading us to be defiant and rebellious. Whenever those in position of power over us use power against us, our natural distrust is reinforced and hardened.

Decisions to defy authority, including disobeying God's instructions, always involve (1) a desire for more, (2) the belief that the more can be had through a different way than what has been laid out, and (3) trusting of one's self and one's wisdom over the person in authority, including God.

The issue of authority is an issue of trust.

The Woman Took ... Ate ... Gave

The woman's actions are described in simple terms: she took ... ate ... and gave. Her actions grew out of and gave expression to the choice she had made to trust her own wisdom rather than follow the instructions given to the couple by the LORD God.

The description of what the woman did brings to mind the description of what Jesus did with the Passover meal he shared with his disciples on the night of his arrest. "While they were eating, Jesus *took* a loaf of bread, and after blessing it he broke it, and *gave* it to the disciples, and said, 'Take, *eat*; this is my body" (Matthew 26:26, emphasis added). Jesus took, blessed, gave, and invited the disciples to eat.

The contrast is stark. The fruit of the tree was forbidden; the bread Jesus broke was freely given. The woman willfully took of the fruit of the tree; Jesus willingly took the bread and the broken body it foretold. The LORD God's instructions were given with a warning of consequences; Jesus's instructions were an invitation to receive a gift. When the woman ate, her eyes were opened to her nakedness, stirring shame and fear. Eating the bread today in Holy Communion opens our eyes to the self-giving love of God and to the grace with which God embraces us. When the woman (and man) took and ate, she experienced brokenness, alienation, and death. When we take and eat, we open our lives to healing, reconciliation, and life.

What Is It That You Have Done

It's not my fault!

When confronted with what they had done, both the man and the woman sought to avoid responsibility for it. The man blamed the woman; the woman blamed the serpent.

Seeking to avoid responsibility for a situation by blaming others is a part of our human condition. We are natural blame-shifters. In our attempt to avoid the pain of facing our wrongdoing, we point the finger at someone else.

Blaming compounds the wrong. It prevents the resolution that is needed if we are to move beyond the wrongdoing. It keeps us stuck in the fear, guilt, and shame spawned by the wrongdoing.

Blaming others is a form of self-deception. It is a way of deflecting the truth about ourselves. It is an attempt to avoid personal responsibility for our own life. Blaming is evidence of a split deep within our psyche. It reflects a lack of wholeness deep within. This internal brokenness is yet another characteristic of our human condition.

Self-awareness and the willingness to be self-responsible are essential components in spiritual growth and personal change. They are what help us grow emotionally-relationally-spiritually. Without them, there is no personal growth. A lack of self-awareness and the inability to be self-responsible keep us stuck in emotional and spiritual immaturity.

Healing that leads to wholeness and maturity begins when we take responsibility for our choices, actions, and lives.

The steadfast, faithful love of the LORD—grace—expressed in forgiveness gives us the courage to face the wrong we have done. Trusting God's grace, we claim the forgiveness that is given freely and lavishly. Freed from the pain of guilt and shame, we can then see beyond our wrongdoing to the underlying issues. We can learn from and grow from our experience of failure.

The LORD God in the Story of the Garden

The story of the garden draws a portrait of the LORD God through what God does. The LORD God ...

- created the man, Genesis 2:7;
- created the garden, the animals, and the woman in order to address the man's need, Genesis 2:8, 18—23;
- enjoyed fellowship with the man and the woman, Genesis 3:8;
- looked for and called out to the couple when they hid, Genesis 3:9;

- confronted the man and the woman, calling them out into the light of truth, Genesis 3:11;
- allowed the couple to experience the consequences of their choices, Genesis 3:14—19;
- refused to abandon the couple as they experienced the consequences of their choices, Genesis 3:21—24;
- responded with compassion to them as they dealt with their new reality, Genesis 3:21—24;
- provided garments to cover their nakedness and shame, Genesis 3:21;
- protected them from an endless life lived in brokenness, Genesis 3:22—24.

The portrait of the LORD God in the story of the garden is the portrait of God found throughout the Bible. God is a God of steadfast, faithful love who refused to give up on the people of Israel, even when they rebelled against God. During their experience of exile in Babylon, the story of the garden would have been seen as their story. The couple's expulsion from the garden would have been understood as the loss of their homeland in their exile in Babylon. They would have understood their experience of exile as death. Yet, the story would also have been viewed as a word of hope. Just as the LORD God did not abandon the couple as they experienced the consequences of their choice, so the LORD had not abandoned them. Compare Isaiah 40:27—31.

A Guide for Personal Reflection and Journaling, for Group Conversation and Discussion

1. How do you reconcile human free will and the sovereignty of God? What is your reaction to presentation of these topics in this chapter?
2. What is your understanding of the will of God? What is your reaction to the idea that "the will of God" could be many things?
3. Do you think more in terms of judgment or consequences? Why? What is your reaction to thinking in terms of consequences rather than judgment?

4. How do you explain the presence of evil? What gives you strength and hope in the face of evil? What was your reaction to the presentation about evil in this chapter?

5. Do you identity with the struggle to be human? In what ways do you seek to escape the limitations that are a part of being human? What would it look like for you to make peace with the limitations of being human?

6. In what ways do you struggle with authority? Why? What does that struggle create in your life and relationships?

7. Do you identify with the inclination to avoid responsibility by shifting the blame to others? Who do you commonly blame?

8. What does the story of the garden teach you about the LORD God?

CHAPTER 11

HOW ARE WE TO UNDERSTAND
THE STORY OF THE GARDEN?

M ost readers understand the story of the garden as the story of "The Fall." This understanding is but one way to understand the story.

The Fall

The popular understanding of the story of the garden as "The Fall" developed late in biblical history. It would *not* have been the way the early Hebrew people understood it.[30]

The earliest roots of this understanding are found in the writings of the Jewish apocrypha, dating to the late post-exilic period and after the compilation of the Hebrew Scriptures. One such writing— Ecclesiasticus, also known as the Wisdom of Jesus Son of Sirach— states, "From a woman sin had its beginning, and because of her we all die" (Sirach 25:24).[31] The book of Sirach has the most negative view of women found in any Jewish writing. This viewpoint is echoed in 1 Timothy 2:13—15.[32]

This understanding was reinforced by Augustine of Hippo (born 345 C.E.). Augustine converted to Christianity after an early life of excessive sexual indulgence. He entered the priesthood and eventually became a bishop in North Africa. Using the story of the garden, Augustine introduced the idea of original sin. He taught sin was passed down biologically through our mothers. Because of original sin, he taught, all are utterly helpless, totally dependent upon God for salvation. The concept of original sin became a central doctrine in John Calvin's teachings during the Reformation of the 1500's. His teachings, which bear his name—Calvinism, have been carried on and are found today in Presbyterian theology.

Viewing the story of the garden as "The Fall" was made popular by John Milton's widely read poem "Paradise Lost," published in England during the mid-1600's. The poem shaped the theology of the lay people in England and found its way into American thinking through immigrants from England. The poem has shaped conservative, evangelical theology in the United States.

Understanding the story of the garden as "The Fall" is not supported by the teachings of the Christian Scriptures nor would it have been the way the early Hebrew people understood the story when it first became a part of their scriptures.

Reading the Story of the Garden with Jewish Eyes

A guide to understanding the story of the garden is to read it from the perspective of the early Hebrew people when the story first became a part of their scriptures. Such a perspective leads us to ask: "What was the story's message for the early Hebrews in their exile and post-exile situation?"

As we attempt to approach the story of the garden from this perspective, we remember that Hebrew scholars have traditionally avoided making a single interpretation of their scriptures. They always leave the door open to additional, different understandings that are applicable to different situations. This practice is known as Midrash. A collection of such teachings is found in the Jewish Talmud. In keeping with this tradition, Jewish interpreters offer a variety of ways of understanding the story of the garden. These differing understandings focus on different parts of the story.

One understanding focuses on the man's role in relation to the earth. This focus leads to an understanding that emphasizes our responsibility to care of the earth and of creation. Genesis 2:5 specifically mentions the lack of plants and herbs because "there was no one to till the ground." The story ends with the man being sent from the garden "to till the ground from which he was taken" (Genesis 3:23).

Another understanding of the story centers on the issue of nakedness. Before the deception, nakedness was not an issue. The man and the woman were both naked and felt no shame. Awareness of their nakedness produced shame, fear, and hiding. The story ends with the LORD God providing garments of skin to cover their nakedness. This focus understands the story as a reference to the beginning of human culture.

The theological statement about marriage at the end of Part One (Genesis 2:24) is another focus that leads to yet another understanding. The loss of the garden meant the loss of eternal life. Given that reality, children were the way one lived on beyond death. This focus is expressed in Adam's naming of Eve "because she was the mother of all living" (Genesis 3:20). Life continued through her. This understanding is seen in the genealogies found in the book of Genesis (and elsewhere) as well as in the ancient Hebrew practice of Levirate marriage stipulated in Deuteronomy 25:5—10. This practice is the background to the story of Ruth and Boaz told in the book of Ruth.

The story of the garden can also be understood as a description of the natural emotional development of the individual. The Genesis 2 description of the man and woman in their nakedness reflects the stage of innocence. This stage is a time when life is simple. Fear is not a shaping factor. But innocence gives way to self-awareness. Self-awareness produces a change in how we relate to others, including hiding from others. We hide those things about ourselves that might elicit condemnation and judgment. The story details what life is like after gaining self-awareness. This understanding does not attach any sense of moral failure, i.e. sin, to the story.

When the interpreter's focus is the tree of the knowledge of good and evil and the instructions-prohibition associated with it, the story is understood as a statement about human free will (as described in the previous chapter).

The story ends with the couple sent out of the garden and an angelic guard set to keep them from reentering it. Focusing on this part of the story leads us to understand the garden as representing the place of fellowship with the LORD God. The LORD God and the couple dwelled together in the garden. In the garden, heaven—the dwelling place of God in Hebrew understanding—and earth—the dwelling place of humans—were united. The spiritual and the physical dimensions of life were joined together in a shared mutuality. The spiritual dimension could be experienced directly through the physical senses. The couple enjoyed face to face fellowship with the LORD God. They heard the sound of the LORD God walking in the garden (Genesis 3:8).

The couple's act of disobedience fractured this shared mutuality. Expelled from the garden, they no longer enjoyed the face to face fellowship with the LORD God. Their ability to directly experience the spiritual realm through their physical senses ended. The spiritual and the physical realms were divided, at least from the human perspective. An angel and a flaming sword blocked access back into the garden. A veil now separated the spiritual from the physical realm.[33]

This separation was reflected in the construction of the Tabernacle. A veil separated the Holy Place where the priests served from the Holy of Holies where the LORD, symbolized by the Ark of the Covenant, dwelled. No one was permitted to enter the Holy of Holies except the High Priest. He alone was allowed to enter once a year, on the Day of Atonement, by means of the blood of a sacrificed lamb.

The Hebrew people envisioned a time when this fracture of the spiritual-physical shared mutuality would be healed. Then, heaven and earth would once again be united. The shared mutuality of the spiritual and physical realms would be restored. Peace would permeate all of creation, extending even into the animal kingdom where the relationships found in the garden would be restored (see Isaiah 10:33— 11:9 and 65:17—25). This healing would be the work of God.

The story reflects our modern, scientifically oriented practice of dividing the world into the physical and the spiritual, the secular and the sacred. The angel and sword guarding the way to the tree of life represent a veil that prevents us from seeing the spiritual dimension of life.[34] A metaphor commonly found in scripture is "ears that do not hear and eyes that do not see." We humans are prone to be consumed with physical needs (see Jesus's teaching about worry in Matthew 6:25—34) and our ego-based desires. Such preoccupation blinds us to the spiritual dimension of life, to the kingdom of God Jesus proclaimed, and to the work of God in our lives. This common aspect of our human condition elicits the commands often found in scripture to "Wake up!" and "Stay awake!" Living in the awareness of spiritual realities sets the spiritual person apart from the unspiritual (see 1 Corinthians 2:14—16).

Each of these understandings approaches the story from a different perspective, viewing it through a different lens (focus). Each, in turn, reflects the genius of the use of story in relating truth. Stories touch so many different aspects of our human experience. No one aspect can fully describe what it means to be human. Each lens (focus) and the understanding it produces is needed as we contemplate our human condition.

Reading the Story of the Garden from the Perspective of the Exile

The Hebrew Scriptures began to be collected and compiled during the people's experience of exile in Babylon. This compilation of stories, writings, laws, and poetry became a new source of identity filling the void left by the destruction of the Temple with its sacrificial system and the destruction of the monarchy with its Davidic covenant. By 200 B.C.E., the project had been completed and translated into Greek, the universal language of the day. This Greek version—known as the Septuagint—would have been known and possibly used by both Jesus and the early church.

The Hebrew Scriptures became a central feature in the life of the synagogue. Rabbis taught it to young boys, using it to teach them to read and write. (Typically, Jewish women were not taught the scriptures or how to read or write.) Each Sabbath, the Hebrew Scriptures were systematically read during synagogue worship. Each service included readings from the Law, the Prophets, and the Psalms.[35]

The development of the Hebrew Scriptures raises the question: "How would the Hebrew people living during the Exile and post-exilic periods have understood the story of the garden?"

The story of the garden is the story of Israel, repeated over again and again. It embodies the theology of Deuteronomy by which they interpreted their experience of exile. Israel enjoyed God's favor—in the covenant, in the gift of the land, in the gift of the Law, in the gift of the Tabernacle-Temple, in the gift of the Davidic covenant—as did the man and woman in the garden. Israel rebelled, as did the man and the woman. Deuteronomistic history (Joshua, Judges, 1 & 2 Samuel, 1 & 2 Kings) details this recurring rebellion and its consequences. Israel was exiled into Babylon, driven out of their land, just as Adam and Eve were sent out of the garden. The story of the garden was their story, the story of their experience of exile.[36]

But What about Sin?

Isn't the story of the garden about how sin entered the world? Doesn't it teach that we humans are sinful beings?

Nowhere in the story is the word *sin* used. The word sin does not appear until the story of Cain and Abel. There, it is used by the LORD God as a warning to Cain.

But wasn't the couple's eating of the forbidden fruit the first expression of sin?

The story of the garden reflects a pattern that is inherent to our human condition. It reflects the pattern of Israel's history. In addition, it reflects the pattern of our lives. Although it does not specifically speak of sin, it tells a story to which we all can relate—a story of self-will that leads to the failure to trust that leads to an act of disobedience. In what it relates, the story can help us understand the phenomenon we call sin.

What we call *sin* is inseparably tied to human free will. It is called *free* will because our will is not coerced or dictated by an outside force. It is not overpowered by the sovereignty of God (as we saw in Chapter 10). Our will is ours and ours alone. Free will refers to our ability to choose. We have the option to faithfully obey, but we also have the option to disobey. The two options are inseparable. We identify with the story because we each can identify a time when we chose to disobey the directions we had been given by a person in a position of authority.

What we call *sin* is inseparably tied to our relationship with authority and/or to someone in a position of authority. Sin implies disobedience to a directive.

At its core, what we call *sin* is about trust. Do we trust the person in the position of authority to have our best interest in mind? The serpent's tactic with the woman was to undermine her trust of God, of God's provision, of God's intention, and, thereby, of God's trustworthiness. What we call sin ultimately boils down to "Are we willing to surrender our ability to choose to the directives of another?"

Thus, what we call *sin* is essentially relational. We commonly speak of sin as wrongful behavior. But before it is behavior, it is about relationship with another.

What we call *sin* is more than an act of disobedience. It is first an attitude that gives birth to the act of disobedience. The underlying attitude is one of self-reliance.[37] We rely on our own wisdom rather than trusting the wisdom behind the directive. The LORD God's directive about not eating of the fruit of the tree of the knowledge of good and evil was an attempt to protect the couple: "for in the day that you eat of it you shall die" (Genesis 2:17). The woman chose to follow her own wisdom rather than the directive from the LORD God: "when the woman saw that the tree was good for food, and that it was a delight to the eye, and that the tree was to be desired to make one wise …" (Genesis 3:6). The attitude of self-reliance produces a spirit of rebellion. The spirit of rebellion leads to the act of disobedience. In our efforts to deal with the issue of sin, we must go beyond a focus on an act of disobedience, that is, on behavior. We can only make progress in our efforts by dealing with the underlying attitude of self-reliance that is expressed in a spirit of rebellion.

When we focus on sin as behavior, we are drawn into the age-old pattern of comparing behavior. We avoid dealing with our own failures by focusing on the failures of others that we perceive to be greater than ours. This pattern underlies Jesus's command to not judge others (Matthew 7:1—5). It is seen in the story as both the man and the woman sought to avoid responsibility for what they had each done by blaming another. The man blamed the woman; the woman blamed the serpent.

The story shows that our attitude of self-reliance, our spirit of rebellion, and our acts of disobedience are rooted in fear. The woman, following the serpent's suggestion, was afraid she was missing out on something greater. She wanted the more she thought she was missing, i.e., knowing good from evil like God (Genesis 3:6). This deeply rooted fear produces a self-centered, self-serving spirit. We look out of "ole #1."

The story suggests that the harsh reality and pain of life are the results of our acts of disobedience, what we call *sin*. These realities are not a part of God's design or will. The story shows that living out of self-reliance rather than faithful obedience to God results in shame, fear, hiding, blaming, broken relationships, alienation, and a broken world.

What we call *sin* places us in need of mercy and grace.

The story reminds us that God does not abandon us to the consequences of our choices. The LORD does not react to our self-reliant, rebellious, acts of disobedience. Rather, the LORD relates to us out of the overflowing abundance of steadfast love and faithfulness that lie at the heart of the divine character. Consequently, we are not left with just the negative consequences of what we chose. God continues to work for our good.

The resolution of what we call *sin* comes from God through Christ and the work of the Spirit. Such is the story of salvation that is greater than the story of the garden. It is the story told in the rest of scripture.

A Guide for Personal Reflection and Journaling, for Group Conversation and Discussion

1. What reaction do you have to the idea that the garden story is not the story of "The Fall?" What makes it difficult to view it differently?
2. What is your reaction to the "reading with Jewish eyes" section?
3. How does the perspective of the Jewish experience of exile change how the story is understood?
4. What is your "take away" from the "But What About Sin?" section?

CHAPTER 12

THE STORY OF THE GARDEN
IN THE NEW TESTAMENT

The story of the garden is found in the earliest chapters of the Hebrew Scriptures—Genesis 2 and 3. It resurfaces in the last two chapters of the Christian Scriptures—Revelation 21—22.

The book of Revelation is a style of writing known as apocalyptic literature. It was a style of literature that was popular in the life of Israel between 250 B.C.E. to 200 C.E. This kind of literature can be found in the Hebrew Scriptures in portions of Ezekiel, Daniel, Joel, and a small section of Isaiah. In the Apocrypha, this style of writing is found in The Book of Enoch, The Assumption of Moses, The Secrets of Enoch, The Book of Baruch, and the Book of 4 Ezra. In addition to the book of Revelation, Jesus's temple discourse (Mark 13:1—37 and Luke 21:5—36) is an example of this kind of literature in the New Testament.

A central characteristic of apocalyptic literature was the use of symbols and imagery, including the use of numbers as symbols. The symbols were used to reveal and to conceal. Those to whom the apocalypse was written would know the symbols and understand the message they communicated. To those persecuting the faithful and causing the suffering, the symbols would appear to be meaningless nonsense.

In interpreting apocalyptic literature, we must move beyond the symbol to its meaning. The symbols are not to be understood literally.

The last two chapters of Revelation are the final vision in the book. The vision consists of three images: a new heaven and a new earth (Revelation 21:1—8), a new Jerusalem within that new creation (Revelation 21:9—27), and a new garden (Revelation 22:1—5). This vision is the fulfillment of the Hebrew people's vision of the reuniting of heaven and earth. These final chapters in Revelation draw heavily on images found in the story of the garden.

The first image of a new creation is drawn from Isaiah 65:17—25. That text describes a new creation and a new Jerusalem that no longer experience war and are freed from the ravages of war. The result is universal peace:

> The wolf and the lamb shall feed together,
> the lion shall eat straw like the ox;
> but the serpent—its food shall be dust!
> They shall not hurt or destroy on all my holy mountain,
> says the LORD" (Isaiah 65:25).

Note the reference to the serpent, an image from the story of the garden. This new creation is described as a place when God once again dwells in fellowship with humans (Revelation 21:3) as the LORD God did with the couple in the story of the garden. In this new creation, everything is made new (Revelation 21:5). The pain, death, and crying associated with the story of the garden are all removed. The first things—the brokenness, alienation, and curse found in the story of the garden—"have passed away" (Revelation 21:4b). "And the one who was seated on the throne (God) said, 'See, I am making all things new'" (Revelation 21:5). God is creating again. God is fashioning a new creation that is not marred by shame, fear, hiding, blaming, and brokenness.

The image of the new Jerusalem draws from the book of Ezekiel and the breastplate of the high priest. It is portrayed as a cube, the symbol of perfection for the Hebrew people. It is the place of perfect fellowship with God.

The image of a new garden makes seven different references to the story of the garden and the story that follows it.

The first reference is to "the river of the water of life, bright as crystal, flowing from the throne of God and of the Lamb the middle of the street" (Revelation 22:1—3). The river calls to mind the river flowing out of Eden, dividing into four branches around which civilizations flourished (Genesis 2:10). This life-giving river flows from the throne of God and the Lamb. God and the Son (in Revelation, the Lamb represents Jesus) are the source of life.

The second reference is the tree of life. The man and woman were sent out of the garden to keep them from taking of the tree of life and living eternally in their broken state (Genesis 3:22—23). In the new garden, the tree is readily available year round. It produces twelve kinds of fruit, one for each month. In Revelation, the number twelve is the symbol for the people of God, i.e., the twelve tribes of Israel and the twelve apostles. The image suggests that eternal life is found in covenant relationship with God.

In the story of the garden, the man and woman used fig leaves to cover their nakedness and the shame they felt. They hid from one another behind fig leaves. In the new garden, leaves are for healing: "the leaves of the tree are for the healing of the nations" (Revelation 22:2). The shame is healed and the fear it produced is removed. The leaves suggest the grace and forgiveness with which God deals with our sin.

The fourth reference to the story of the garden is to the curse that was placed on the serpent and the ground as a consequence of the couple's choice to disobey the directive of the LORD God, trust their own wisdom, and take of the fruit of the tree of the knowledge of good and evil. In the new garden, the curse no longer exists. "Nothing accursed will be found there any more" (Revelation 22:3). The story of Noah and the flood is told against the backdrop of the desire for relief from the curse placed on the ground (Genesis 5:28—29). That relief is found in the new garden through the redemptive work of the Lamb.

In the story of the garden, the man and the woman hid from the presence of the LORD God after partaking of the forbidden fruit (Genesis 3:8). In the new garden, the people of God enjoy face-to-face fellowship with God. "They will see his face" (Revelation 22:4). The image suggests openness and intimacy. Hiding is replaced with freedom to know and be known. Broken relationship with God is replaced with unhindered relationship.

The sixth reference is to the story of Cain that follows the story of the garden. In the Cain story, the LORD placed a mark on Cain's forehead to protect him from retaliation for the murder of his brother Abel (Genesis 4:15). In the new garden, the people of God are marked with the name of God (Revelation 22:4). That name speaks of more than protection. They are the people of God who live in relationship with God. They belong to God.

The final reference to the Genesis texts is found in Revelation 22:5, "And there will be no more night; they need no light of lamp or sun, for the Lord God will be their light, and they will reign forever and ever." In the story of creation, the man and woman are given dominion over the fish, birds, cattle, wild animals, and every creeping thing (Genesis 1:26). They reign over creation. In the story of the garden, the man gave names to the different animals (Genesis 2:19). The naming reflects the man's authority over them. He reigned over the garden and over the animals in the garden. In the new garden, the people of God reign with the Risen Christ in victory over sin and death.

Three themes run through each of these three images—a new creation, a new Jerusalem, a new garden. In each image, relationship and fellowship with God has been restored. God dwells in the midst of God's people just as the LORD God shared the garden with the man and the woman. In that restored relationship, the people of God walk in the light of God (Revelation 21:22—24; 22:5). They no longer trust their wisdom over God's directives. They no longer live out of a spirit of self-reliance but live in glad dependence upon God. They no longer live out of a spirit of defiance but they live in joyful trust of God. They no longer follow their own ways but live the ways of God. Because of this restored relationship, the destructive consequences of refusing to live in faithful obedience have been forever removed.

Genesis 2 describes life in the garden. It reflects how we long for life to be. The three images found in Revelation 21 and 22 reflect that same reality.

A Guide for Personal Reflection and Journaling, for Group Conversation and Discussion

1. What is your "take away" from this chapter?
2. How does this explanation of Revelation 21—22 impact your understanding of heaven?

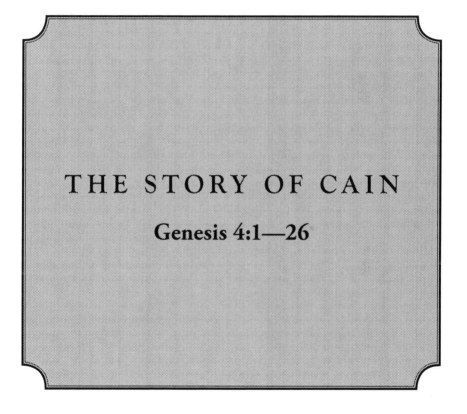

THE STORY OF CAIN

Genesis 4:1—26

Genesis 4:1—26

N ow the man knew his wife Eve, and she conceived and bore Cain, saying, "I have produced a man with the help of the LORD." ²Next she bore his brother Abel. Now Abel was a keeper of sheep, and Cain a tiller of the ground.

³In the course of time Cain brought to the LORD an offering of the fruit of the ground, ⁴and Abel for his part brought of the firstlings of his flock, their fat portions. And the LORD had regard for Abel and his offering, ⁵but for Cain and his offering he had no regard. So Cain was very angry, and his countenance fell.

⁶The LORD said to Cain, "Why are you angry, and why has your countenance fallen? ⁷If you do well, will you not be accepted? And if you do not do well, sin is lurking at the door; its desire is for you, but you must master it."

⁸Cain said to his brother Abel, "Let us go out to the field." And when they were in the field, Cain rose up against his brother Abel, and killed him.

⁹Then the LORD said to Cain, "Where is your brother Abel?" He said, "I do not know; am I my brother's keeper?" ¹⁰And the LORD said, "What have you done? Listen; your brother's blood is crying out to me from the ground! ¹¹And now you are cursed from the ground, which has opened its mouth to receive your brother's blood from your hand. ¹²When you till the ground, it will no longer yield to you its strength; you will be a fugitive and a wanderer on the earth."

¹³Cain said to the LORD, "My punishment is greater than I can bear! ¹⁴Today you have driven me away from the soil, and I shall be hidden from your face; I shall be a fugitive and a wanderer on the earth, and anyone who meets me may kill me." ¹⁵Then the LORD said to him, "Not so! Whoever kills Cain will suffer a sevenfold vengeance." And the LORD put a mark on Cain, so that no one who came upon him would kill him.

¹⁶Then Cain went away from the presence of the LORD, and settled in the land of Nod, east of Eden.

¹⁷Cain knew his wife, and she conceived and bore Enoch; and he built a city, and named it Enoch after his son Enoch. ¹⁸To Enoch was born Irad; and Irad was the father of Mehujael, and Mehujael the father of Methushael, and Methushael the father of Lamech.

[19]Lamech took two wives; the name of the one was Adah, and the name of the other Zillah. [20]Adah bore Jabal; he was the ancestor of those who live in tents and have livestock. [21]His brother's name was Jubal; he was the ancestor of all those who play the lyre and pipe. [22]Zillah bore Tubal-cain, who made all kinds of bronze and iron tools. The sister of Tubal-cain was Naamah.

[23]Lamech said to his wives: "Adah and Zillah, hear my voice; you wives of Lamech, listen to what I say: I have killed a man for wounding me, a young man for striking me. [24]If Cain is avenged sevenfold, truly Lamech seventy-sevenfold."

[25]Adam knew his wife again, and she bore a son and named him Seth, for she said, "God has appointed for me another child instead of Abel, because Cain killed him." [26]To Seth also a son was born, and he named him Enosh. At that time people began to invoke the name of the LORD.

CHAPTER 13

INTRODUCING THE STORY OF CAIN

The story of the garden came to an end with the LORD God sending the man and woman out of the garden. But the story continues with the story of Cain.

Traditionally, the story is known as the story of Cain and Abel. I have chosen to refer to the story as the story of Cain. Cain is the main character of the story. Abel is a secondary character. This secondary role is reflected in how his birth is referenced in relation to Cain. Abel is Cain's brother. Abel is a necessary part of the story but not its focus. Cain is center stage. It is his story.

The story of Cain is linked to the story of the garden. The man and the woman—the main (and only human) characters in the story of the garden—are used to introduce the story of Cain. But the story of Cain stands alone. It reflects life after the garden and the continuing impact of the couple's decision to not live in faithful obedience to the LORD God.

Like the story of the garden, the story of Cain is the kind of story that would have been passed down by word of mouth and told around a fire in the evening. It does not bear the scholarly touches found in the story of creation in Genesis 1. Its structure flows out of its storyline:

> 4:1—2, the birth of Cain and his brother Abel
> 4:3—7, Cain's anger
> 4:8, Cain's murder of his brother Abel
> 4:9—12, the LORD's confrontation of Cain and the consequences of Cain's sin
> 4:13—15, Cain's lament and the mark of Cain

4:16, Cain settled in the land of Nod
4:17—24, the genealogy of Cain
4:25—26, the birth of Seth.

Though tied to the story of the garden, the story of Cain comes from a different source. The name used to speak of God in the story of Cain is different from the name used in the story of the garden. This difference points to a different source.[38] In the story of the garden, the name "the LORD God" is used to speak of God. The story of Cain uses the name "the LORD". This name is the Hebrew name YWH, the covenant name of God. It is the name used in the Exodus story which culminated in the covenant at Sinai (see Exodus 3:1—14). Scholars identify the stories that use the name "the LORD" as originating out of the southern kingdom of Judah.

The story of Cain ends with his genealogy (Genesis 4:17-24) and the story of the birth of his brother Seth (Genesis 4:25-26).

CHAPTER 14

LIFE AFTER THE GARDEN: THE STORY OF CAIN

T he story of the garden graphically portrays the consequences of choosing not to live in faithful obedience in relationship with the LORD God. The story of Cain shows how those consequences were compounded in life after the garden.

The Birth of Cain and His Brother Abel, Genesis 4:1—2

The story of Cain begins with the story of his conception and birth. The reference to the man and his wife Eve (Genesis 4:1) ties his story to the story of the garden. Thus, the story of Cain is the story of life after the garden.

From the outset, the story draws a contrast between the two brothers. The contrast is made in how their births are referenced, in the names they are given, and in the vocations each chose.

The account of Cain's birth is elaborate in comparison to the account of his brother's birth. It begins by referring to his conception after the man "knew his wife Eve" (Genesis 4:1). Eve viewed his birth as the work of the LORD: "I have produced a man with the help of the LORD" (Genesis 4:1). She saw his birth as a marvelous act of creation mirroring the creative acts of God. The Hebrew word translated "produced" can be translated as "to bring into being, to create, to bring forth, to produce." Eve viewed Cain's birth as a creative act in which life was brought into being—not unlike God's work of bringing life into being when God created the world.

In contrast to the description of Cain's birth, the birth of Abel is simply noted. "Next she bore his brother Abel" (Genesis 4:2). Abel is identified as "his brother." His identity is tied to Cain. Clearly, the focus of the story is Cain. Abel is only important in relationship to Cain. The elaborate description of Cain's birth coupled with the reserved mention of Abel's birth reflects the joy and hope associated with the birth of a firstborn son in a family. No other son born into the family receives the kind of focus or love the firstborn son receives. The firstborn establishes the family line and guarantees the continuation of the father's life through his descendants.[39]

The name Abel means "breath, vanity." It implies frailty and weakness, that which is fleeting. The name Cain is a play on the word "produced" that Eve used to speak of his birth. His name pointed to the creative, life-giving act of birth. It implies strength. The name Cain introduces irony into the story. Cain, whose name refers to a creative, life-giving act, becomes the one who destroys life by killing his brother. His name points to the miracle of birth yet he is known for causing the first death. His strength was not used as God uses strength, to create and bless. His strength was used to rob another of his life.

Cain followed in the footsteps of his father Adam. He was a farmer who tilled the ground. Abel, mentioned first in verse 2 although he is the second born, was a shepherd. The difference in their vocations sets the stage for rest of the story.

The contrast between the two brothers raises the question: how do we deal with one who is different? How do we deal with one who is not like me? The two were brothers, yet they were different. How do we view the ways we are different? The difference can be seen as God's design and thereby a gift or the difference can be viewed as a threat to be feared and eliminated. The story of Cain reflects our natural inclination to fear the one who is different.

Cain's Anger, Genesis 4:3—7

After the brief introduction setting up the story, the narrative moves quickly to the central movement of the story: Cain's anger, leading to the murder of his brother.

Cain's anger was his reaction to the LORD's response to the offerings each brother brought. Each brought an offering out of what their work in their respective vocations had produced. Cain, the farmer, brought an offering of "the fruit of the ground;" Abel, the keeper of sheep, offered a gift from "the firstlings of his flock, their fat portions" (Genesis 4:34). The story offers no explanation of why the offerings were made. It reports the gifts as though such offerings were a normal part of their lives.

"And the LORD had regard for Abel and his offering, but for Cain and his offering he had no regard" (Genesis 4:b—5a). This statement about the LORD's response to the two offerings interrupts the natural progression of the story—detail followed by detail. It grabs the listener's attention, drawing him deeper into the story. The story is suddenly infused with heightened emotion.

The Hebrew word translated as "had regard for" means "to look on, to recognize and take note of, to pay attention to and thereby to value." Thus, to not regard something would be to ignore it, treating it as insignificant and unimportant. The LORD valued Abel and his offering but not Cain and his offering.

The text gives no explanation for the LORD's reaction to either offering. Some attempt to explain the LORD's response by focusing on the offering itself. Abel's offering was of the firstlings and their fat portions, i.e., their best parts, whereas Cain's offering did not indicate anything special about it. It was just the fruit of the ground. Abel's offering was of the better parts of the flock and, thus, were viewed as a better offering. Others explain the LORD's response by focusing on the brothers themselves. The text uses the language "for Abel and his offering" and "for Cain and his offering." This explanation assumes something about the brothers' attitude in giving their offerings. Both explanations are speculations as the story does not give a reason for the LORD's response. In addition, both explanations assume God relates to us out of who we are and what we do. Our desire to know the "why" behind the LORD's response arises out of merit-based thinking. We want an answer so that we can do what is pleasing and, thereby, gain the LORD's favor. The witness of scripture is God relates to us out of who God is, not in reaction to who we are or what we do. The LORD's response to the two offerings had nothing to do with either who the two brothers were or what they did.

When a text does not answer the questions we ask, we are asking the wrong questions. Our unanswered questions lead us to speculate. In doing so, we move away from the story itself and what it teaches. We are better served recognizing and acknowledging the text does not address the questions we have so that we can give our attention to what the story does say.

And so we come to Cain's anger. "So Cain was very angry, and his countenance fell" (Genesis 4:5b). Cain burned with anger. He was angry with the LORD. He was especially angry with his brother.

How are we to understand Cain's anger? What happened emotionally and relationally when the LORD did not have regard for Cain's offering?

When the LORD had regard for Abel's offering but not his, Cain was displaced. His brother, who had always lived in his shadow, now received the spotlight to which he (Cain) was accustomed. Abel's offering was valued while his was not. In that reversal of fortune, Cain lost his sense of place and standing, his sense of significance and importance. The first became last and the last became first. Probably for the first time, Cain experienced what it was like to feel *less than*. And he didn't like it. As the firstborn, he was accustomed to being valued over others.

Cain's intense anger reflected this loss of standing. That loss of standing changed how he viewed his brother Abel. His brother had become a competitor. He was a threat.

Cain withdrew inside himself, brooding on his pain and stoking his anger. "And his countenance fell" (Genesis 4:5). The Hebrew wording means his head hung. His eyes were downcast. He looked at no one. His face and body language reflected what was going on inside his mind. With his head hung, he refused to look up. He could not see anything but his own perspective. He thought of nothing but his own pain. He could not value anyone but himself. He was totally self-absorbed.

But the LORD did not indulge Cain's moodiness. Instead, the LORD spoke to him, calling him out of his self-absorbed thoughts, challenging him to deal with his anger, inviting him to learn from it, warning him about the danger he faced if he failed to do so, encouraging him to be strong, offering him a way back. "Why are you angry, and why has your countenance fallen? If you do well, will you not be accepted? And if you do not do well, sin is lurking at the door; its desire is for you, but you must master it" (Genesis 4:6—7). The LORD's confrontation was an act of compassion. The LORD sought to help Cain deal with the pain that was expressed through his emotion. The LORD sought to protect Cain from the precipice on which he stood.

The way the LORD confronted Cain was by asking questions. The question "Why are you angry?" (Genesis 4:6) called Cain to reflect on what he was feeling (self-reflection). Self-reflection produces self-awareness. Self-awareness is a prerequisite to exercising self-control (self-management). Self-control is the way we grow and change.

"If you do well … if you do not do well" (Genesis 4:7) called Cain to exercise self-control. "If you do well" was *not* a reference to: Cain's offering. Rather, the statement was a reference to how Cain was reacting in the situation. "If you do well" was a call to consciously choose what he would do rather than simply reacting out of anger.

The LORD was more concerned with Cain's reaction and choices than with his offering. Ultimately, the LORD was attempting to get Cain to move beyond seeing his brother as a competitor. The LORD wanted him to value Abel as a brother. But in order to view Abel differently, Cain would have to learn from his anger. He would have to recognize the position of power and privilege he was fighting to protect. He would have to acknowledge the disregard with which he treated Abel.

In this part of the story, the word *sin* is used for the first time in scripture. It is portrayed as a vicious animal or an enemy lying in wait to catch us unaware. Its desire is to possess us.

The LORD warned Cain about the possibility of sin that lay before him. The sin was not his anger.[40] But his experience of anger opened the door to the possibility of sin. It made him vulnerable to sin. Whether anger led to sin depended upon how Cain dealt with it. The LORD's warning affirmed that Cain was not powerless in dealing with sin. Although sin had the power to overwhelm him, he could master it … as can we!

There is no record of Cain's response to God's confrontation. His actions indicate he chose to ignore it.

The story's depiction of Cain's anger is like a mirror in which we can see ourselves and our own experience. That is part of the story's power. Like Cain, we can become consumed with how we perceive we have been wronged. Our pain can blind us to anything but ourselves.

We can become controlled by our emotions, abdicating our power to deal with them. We often fail to see beyond our emotions to the underlying issues, failing to hear what our emotions say to us. Failing to deal with and learn from our emotions, we attack others, dumping our pain on them. Living with little self-awareness and even less self-control, we follow Cain down the path of sin.

Cain's Murder of His Brother Abel, Genesis 4:8

Cain's self-absorbed brooding gave birth to a plot against his brother. It was a simple plan. Get alone with his brother; when they were alone, attack him. His actions were deliberate, planned, and premeditated. He viewed his brother as his rival who had displaced him. In order to regain and secure his place, this competitor had to be eliminated.

"Cain rose up against his brother Abel" like an animal attacking its prey. The sin that was portrayed as a vicious animal waiting to pounce upon its victim (Genesis 4:7) was embodied in Cain's assault on Abel.

This first recorded sin in life after the garden was an act of violence. Violence is the use of power against another in order to overpower and control him or to destroy him. It uses power in a self-serving way. Violence stands in opposition to the way God uses power. As seen in the story of creation, God uses power to create life and nurture it to maturity. God uses power to bring structure and fullness to the empty void of chaos. God uses power to bring about that which is called good, very good. Jesus identified this contrast in how power can be used, teaching his disciples to use power to serve.

> You know that among the Gentiles those whom they recognize as their rulers lord it over them, and their great ones are tyrants over them. But it is not so among you; but whoever wishes to become great among you must be your servant, and whoever wishes to be first among you must be slave of all. For the Son of Man came not to be served but to serve, and to give his life a ransom for many (Mark 10:42—45).

The Gentiles who do not know God or the ways of God "lord it over" as tyrants. They use power over, down against others, for their own benefit at the other's expense. This self-serving way of using power is a part of our human condition. Jesus taught his disciples a radically different way of using power, the way of the servant. A servant uses power the way God uses power: alongside the other for the other's benefit, even at great cost to self.

Following our own wisdom rather than living in faithful obedience to the LORD's directives opens the door to violence. Our self-serving nature, inherent to our human condition, leads us to use our power for our own advantage, often at the expense of another. When we view the other through the eyes of fear, seeing them as a competitor, we use our power to protect ourselves against the threat we believe they represent. When push comes to shove, we use our power to eliminate the threat they pose. We use our power against them, i.e., violently.

The issue of violence will resurface in the introduction to the story of Noah and the flood.

The LORD's Confrontation of Cain and the Consequences of Cain's Sin, Genesis 4:9—12

Even though Cain's murder of his brother was done in secret, it was known by the LORD. The LORD's confrontation of Cain introduces the central theme of the story captured in Cain's question "Am I my brother's keeper?" (Genesis 4:9). What responsibility do those in positions of power and affluence have in relation to "their brother" who is poor, powerless, and vulnerable to exploitation?

In the story of the garden, the LORD God called to the man, "Where are you?" (Genesis 3:9). The story of Cain introduces a second question, "Where is your brother?" (Genesis 4:9). The first question dealt with the man's relationship with God. This second deals with Cain's relationship with his brother. These two questions capture the two relationships that dominate Hebrew thought: one's relationship with God, one's relationship with others. In the New Testament era, these two relationships were viewed as the heart of the Hebrew law.

> One of the scribes came near and heard them disputing with one another, and seeing that (Jesus) answered them well, he asked him, "Which commandment is the first of all?" Jesus answered, "The first is, 'Hear, O Israel: the Lord our God, the Lord is one; you shall

love the Lord your God with all your heart, and with all your soul, and with all your mind, and with all your strength.' The second is this, 'You shall love your neighbor as yourself.' There is no other commandment greater than these." Then the scribe said to him, "You are right, Teacher; you have truly said that 'he is one, and besides him there is no other'; and 'to love him with all the heart, and with all the understanding, and with all the strength,' and 'to love one's neighbor as oneself,' —this is much more important than all whole burnt offerings and sacrifices" (Mark 12:28—33).

Both relationships—with God, with neighbor—are negatively impacted when we fail to live in faithful obedience to the LORD.

"Where is your brother?" is a haunting question for those who hold positions of power, enjoying the privilege and affluence associated with their position. Privilege and affluence have a way of blinding us to those who do not have what we have. We do not see "where" they live— the lack of resources and opportunity, the struggle to just survive much less get ahead, the obstacles they must overcome in order to succeed, the cycle in which the generations are stuck.

Early in the story, the LORD confronted Cain, calling him to deal with his anger. That confrontation was an attempt to protect Cain from sin. Now the LORD confronts Cain again, calling him to deal with his sin. The LORD's question provided an opportunity for Cain to be honest about what he had done, accepting responsibility for his actions. Honesty and the ownership of responsibility are what make reconciliation and healing possible. Apart from honesty—with self, with God, with others—reconciliation and healing are not possible. The refusal to be honest contributes to the alienation.

Cain answered the LORD's question by doing just the opposite. He lied and refused to accept any responsibility for Abel. "I do not know?" (Genesis 4:9). In the story of the garden, the couple hid behind fig leaves. When confronted with what they had done, they attempted to avoid responsibility by blaming another. Here, Cain hid behind a lie. One sin—the murder of his brother Abel—gave birth to a second sin—a lie. Sin gives birth to more sin. In addition to the lie, Cain attempted to avoid any responsibility for his brother. "Am I my brother's keeper?"

Central to the Hebrew people's understanding of God was the LORD's care for others, particularly those who were exploited by others (the oppressed), the powerless (the widows and orphans), and the immigrants who lived as aliens in their midst. To be the people of God was to be responsible for and to others, particularly the poor and powerless (Isaiah 1:17). When we enjoy power, privilege, and affluence, we often live as though we have no responsibility for others.

The LORD did not accept either Cain's lie or his refusal of responsibility for what he had done. With yet another question, the LORD confronted Cain. "What have you done? Listen; your brother's blood is crying out to me from the ground!" (Genesis 4:10). The LORD's words are full of anguish and pain. They called Cain to face the reality he denied. His brother's blood and the ground which received it cried out to the LORD. They called for Cain to be held accountable for what he had done. The LORD called Cain to hear the cries He heard. "Listen!" The command is, once again, the LORD's attempt to help Cain escape his inability to see from any perspective but his own. It was an attempt to get Cain to see how *Abel* was the one who had been wronged, not Cain.

As in the story of the garden, choices have consequences. Cain would have to live with two devastating consequences. The first was in relation to the earth and, thus, in relation to his vocation as a farmer. The second was in relation to his place among others.

"And now you are cursed from the ground, which has opened its mouth to receive your brother's blood from your hand. When you till the ground, it will no longer yield to you its strength" (Genesis 4:11—12). In the story of the Garden, the curse was placed on the ground which produced the trees and vegetation that fed the couple. Here, Cain himself bears the curse. The ground had given of its life to feed Cain the farmer. Cain, in turn, had fed his brother's blood to the ground. The covenant with the soil had been violated. Consequently, the soil would no longer feed Cain. It would withhold its strength from Cain. Cain's life as a farmer was over.

Cain murdered his brother Abel to protect the special standing and place he enjoyed in the family. Abel had become a threat to that standing. The second consequence of Cain's sin was the loss of standing and place with others. He no longer had a place to belong or standing in the eyes of others. "You will be a fugitive and a wanderer on the earth" (Genesis 4:12). In place of his settled life as a farmer, tied to a particular piece of the earth, Cain would live as a fugitive. He would wander without extended family or home or place to belong. He lost the very things he murdered his brother to protect—his place within a family, his standing and value within that family. By not valuing his brother (the powerless), Cain lost his place of value and his standing as the blessed. His loss of place and standing went beyond his immediate family. It was his reality in the larger human family. He lived as a fugitive with no place to belong.

Cain's Lament and the Mark of Cain, Genesis 4:13—15

Cain reacted to the consequences by lamenting. His lament was more than an expression of grief over what he was losing. It was a complaint that the consequences were too great and, therefore, unfair. His reaction was that of a person who was accustomed to power, standing, and privilege. "You can't do that to me! That's not fair!"

Understandably, Cain felt overwhelmed by the prospects of what he was facing. "My punishment is greater than I can bear!" (Genesis 4:13). Perhaps for the first time in his life, he felt powerless and vulnerable. Ironically, he was now in the position of his brother Abel—powerless, vulnerable, and not valued.

Cain's lament-complaint was four-fold.

The first lament-complaint was about the loss of his vocation as a farmer and, therein, his livelihood. "Today you have driven me away from the soil" (Genesis 4:14). That which he had inherited from his father and the only thing he had ever known was being taken away from him.

His second lament-complain was the loss of his relationship with the LORD. "I shall be hidden from your face" (Genesis 4:14). Interestingly, his relationship with the LORD was not mentioned as one of the consequences of his sin. Cain assumed that being a fugitive, wandering the earth, also meant being alienated and separated from the LORD, the source of life and blessing.

Cain's third lament-complaint was about being a fugitive wandering the earth. He would have no place that was home. He would have no place of safety. He would have no place where he was known and valued.

His final lament-complaint was his sense of vulnerability and the fear it stirred. "And anyone who meets me may kill me" (Genesis 4:14).

He lived in fear of others and what they would do to him. He expected the worse. They would do to him what he had done to his brother Abel. They would kill him. Such prospects, fueled by his fear, made his sense of being powerless and helpless even greater.

Just as the LORD God did not abandon the couple as they experienced the consequences of their choice, so the LORD did not abandon Cain. The LORD responded to Cain's anguish with the promise of protection. The LORD did not—could not—protect Cain from the consequences of his sin, but God could provide protection in the midst of them.

"Then the LORD said to him, 'Not so! Whoever kills Cain will suffer a sevenfold vengeance.' And the LORD put a mark on Cain, so that no one who came upon him would kill him" (Genesis 4:15). The mark was given to protect Cain from what others might do to him.[41] Just as the LORD was the advocate for Abel in his powerless position, so now God was the advocate and protector of Cain in his vulnerability.

The LORD spoke of "a sevenfold vengeance." In the Hebrew culture, the number seven was considered to be a divine number. Thus, a sevenfold vengeance referred to a divine consequence. Any attack on Cain would bring divine consequences. What those consequences would be are not identified. The phrase will surface again in Cain's genealogy.

Cain Settled in the Land of Nod, Genesis 4:16

A simple statement brings the primary portion of the story to an end. "Then Cain went away from the presence of the LORD, and settled in the land of Nod, east of Eden" (Genesis 4:16).

In the story of the garden, the man and the woman were driven from the garden. Cain was not driven from the presence of the LORD. Cain made the decision to go away from the presence of the LORD. The statement suggests that Cain no longer lived in relationship with the LORD. This decision to live outside of a relationship with the LORD became a central characteristic in Cain's descendants. It sets up the contrast with Seth and his descendants who chose to live in relationship with the LORD (Genesis 4:26).

Cain settled in the land of Nod. The word "Nod" means "wandering, restlessness." It describes a condition rather than a location. Cain lived in a condition of internal restlessness. His life was marked by a lack of settled-ness or peace. He lived the life of a fugitive.

The Genealogy of Cain, Genesis 4:17—24

The story of Cain ends with the genealogy of Cain. Just as the story of Cain continued the story of the garden, so the genealogy of Cain continues to the story of Cain. In the story of Cain, the consequences found in the story of the garden were compounded. The genealogy of Cain depicts how the consequences of Cain's choices rippled throughout the following generations. The man and woman's choice to not live in faithful obedience to the LORD evolved into, in the story of Cain, Cain's choice to not live in relationship with God. Cain's choice to not live in relationship with God bore bitter fruit in the lives of his descendants. The genealogy of Cain portrays that fruit. Our choices impact more than ourselves. They ripple out into the lives of others, including the generations that follow us.

The genealogies in the book of Genesis follow a consistent pattern: a father is named, followed by the first son that was born to him. The pattern is repeated with each successive generation. An interruption in the pattern calls for special attention.

The genealogy of Cain follows this common pattern for seven generations (starting with Adam). The pattern is disrupted in the first generation and the last. Those interruptions of the pattern indicate special interest and/or a point the author-editor wanted to make.

Just as the man knew his wife Eve and she conceived (Genesis 4:1), so Cain knew his wife and she conceived. The son that was born was named Enoch. A special note is made about Enoch. "And (Cain) built a city, and named it Enoch after his son Enoch" (Genesis 4:17). The building of a city is linked to Cain's life as a fugitive, wandering over the face of the earth. A city represents a place of stability and permanence. A walled city offered safety and provided a sense of security. Cain wanted for his son what he himself did not have. Building a city for his son was Cain's attempt to offset the inner restlessness with which he lived. It was an attempt to blunt the sense of fear and vulnerability that haunted his mind. In keeping with our human nature, Cain sought to address his inner, emotional-relational-spiritual needs through the material world. He built a city.

After the special comment about this first generation, Cain's genealogy followed the common pattern until the birth of Lamech, the fifth generation from Cain, the seventh generation from Adam. The genealogy ends with Lamech although his sons are identified. This ending of the genealogy, coupled with the things that are said about Lamech, indicate the author-editor's point in recording the genealogy is found in Lamech's story.

Lamech's story contains three specific details.

The first detail is about Lamech's two wives. "Lamech took two wives; the name of the one was Adah, and the name of the other Zillah" (Genesis 4:19). Lamech's wives are the first women named in Genesis after Eve. They are also the first reference in scripture to polygamy. Lamech's marriages are a change from the one man-one woman relationship found in Genesis 2:23—24. Polygamy is a feature of male domination. It discounts the woman, putting her in a secondary, one-down position while exalting the man. It reduces marriage to the man's needs and desires with procreation being the woman's primary role. It diminishes the relational nature of the marriage—the delight and joy, the openness and sharing between a man and a woman that is reflected in the Genesis 2 text.

The identification of Lamech's wives leads naturally to an identification of their children. In addition to naming them, the text identifies them as ancestors to people with specific skills and vocations (Genesis 4:20—22). One group was nomadic, their lives built around herding livestock. Another excelled in music, playing the lyre and pipe. A third was known for their skill in making tools out of bronze and iron. Even a daughter was identified (the third woman named in Genesis), a highly unusual feature in genealogies. These descriptions indicate that Cain's descendants made great progress technically and culturally. What is not noted is progress relationally, morally, or spiritually. Polygamy suggests moral regression, not moral advancement. It reflects a marriage relationship shaped by the consequences of the man and woman's disobedience (male domination, Genesis 3:17c) rather than God's design (Genesis 2:23—24).

The key detail of Lamech's story is in what he said to his wives.

> Lamech said to his wives:
> 'Adah and Zillah, hear my voice;
> you wives of Lamech, listen to what I say:

I have killed a man for wounding me,
a young man for striking me.
If Cain is avenged sevenfold,
truly Lamech seventy-sevenfold'" (Genesis 4:23—24).

Lamech's statement is about revenge. He played off of the LORD's promise to protect Cain with sevenfold (divine) vengeance, expanding it from sevenfold to seventy-seven fold. Seventy-seven fold carries the idea of unlimited retaliation. The retaliation exceeds the original offense. A wound is avenged with death. Lamech bragged about blood revenge that had no limits. Cain's act of violence—murdering his brother Abel—gave birth to Lamech's spirit of revenge expressed in unlimited, disproportionate retaliation for any wrong he experienced. Lamech did not need or want the LORD's protection. He would take care of himself and exact his own revenge. Cain's act did not stand alone. Its consequences rippled through his descendants with devastating results.

Nowhere in Cain's genealogy is there a reference to the LORD. Cain chose to not live in relationship with the LORD. "Then Cain went away from the presence of the LORD" (Genesis 4:16). The consequence of that choice, like his choice to kill his brother Abel, cascaded throughout the generations that followed. The name of each of Lamech's sons as well as the name of his daughter incorporates the word "Bal." The word echoes the name of the Canaanite god Baal, suggesting Cain's descendants chose to worship a god other than the LORD.

Although Lamech is the end of Cain's genealogy, his words did not die with him. Jesus picked up his words and transformed them. Lamech swore to avenge himself seventy-seven fold. He spoke of unlimited retaliation. Jesus used Lamech's words to speak of unlimited forgiveness, the opposite of retaliation and vengeance.

> "Then Peter came and said to him, 'Lord, if another member of the church sins against me, how often should I forgive? As many as seven times?' Jesus said to him, 'Not seven times, but, I tell you, seventy-seven times'" (Matthew 18:21—22).

Revenge, retaliation, and violence are characteristic of our human condition, but they are not the ways of God. Forgiveness is.

The Birth of Seth, Genesis 4:25—26

The story of Cain ends with the birth of another brother. The last reference to Cain in his story is to that for which he is known: the murder of his brother.

The account of Seth's birth is like that of the birth of Cain. As with Cain, Eve associated the birth of Seth with the work of God. "God has appointed for me another child instead of Abel, because Cain killed him" (Genesis 4:25). Just as Abel's identity was tied to Cain—"his brother Abel" (Genesis 4:2)—so Seth's identity was tied to Abel's. Seth was viewed as a replacement for Abel.

It is difficult to have a sense of one's own self when your identity is tied to another. Such is the challenge of those whose birth order was not that of the firstborn child or of an only child. Firstborn children commonly inherit an identity tied to the larger, extended family. It is difficult to escape the identity we were given in our family of origin. We probably never fully break free from it. We only begin to discover who we really are when we answer the question, "Who am I as God's creation and child, not as someone's child or sibling?"

The birth of Seth ties us back to the story of the garden. It also sets up the genealogy that follows. It is an important link between the story of the garden and the next story—the story of Noah. It also draws a contrast between the line of Cain and the line of Seth. Whereas Cain chose not to live in relationship with the LORD, Seth's line intentionally pursued such a relationship. Beginning with Seth's son, "people began to invoke the name of the LORD" (Genesis 4:26).

"The LORD" (YWH) is the name for God associated with the covenant at Mt. Sinai. The tradition that used the name "the LORD" (YWH) traced its origins back to Seth's son Enosh.

This reference draws a contrast to the descendants of Cain. Cain and his descendants seemingly lived without any relationship with the LORD whereas Seth's descendants lived in intentional relationship with the LORD. They invoked the name of the LORD, that is, they prayed to the LORD. The contrast between the two lines is significant. Cain's lineage ended with Lamech who, in spite of his children's successes, was known for his spirit of vengeance expressed in unlimited, disproportionate retaliation. Seth's lineage produced Noah, the key figure in the next story—one who walked with God (Genesis 6:9) and one who was God's partner in protecting all of life from destruction by the flood. And, unlike Cain's lineage, Seth's lineage continued through Noah to Abraham and the beginning of the story of the people of Israel.

Cain walked away from the presence of the LORD, living as a restless fugitive wandering the face of the earth without a place to belong, a place of safety and security, or a place of valued identity. While Cain walked away from the LORD, Seth's line in Enosh walked in relationship with the LORD. Enosh prayed to the LORD.

Cain is known for what he did. He murdered his brother. In the biblical narrative, Cain is also known for what he did not do. He did not live in relationship with the LORD. The author-editor made a point of that reality.

A Guide for Personal Reflection and Journaling, for Group Conversation and Discussion

1. What new thought or understanding did you experience about the story of Cain?
2. What is your "take away" from the story?
3. With what part(s) of the story can you identify?

CHAPTER 15

MINING THE RICHES OF
THE STORY OF CAIN

Each of the five narratives found in Genesis 1—11 resonate with us because they reflect life as we have experienced it. They are mirrors that allow us to see ourselves and our human condition. They invite us to reflect so that we might learn the great truths they communicate.

Life after the Garden: the Ripple Effect of Sin

The story of the garden recorded the choice by the man and the woman to not live in faithful obedience to the LORD. The story of Cain shows how the consequences of that choice were compounded in life after the garden.

The brokenness in the relationship between the man and the woman evolved in the story of Cain into conflict between brothers, leading one to murder the other. The couple's shame-based fear became, in the story of Cain, a downcast countenance associated with anger. The serpent lured the woman (and the man) into a seemingly spur-of-the-moment decision to disobey the LORD God's directive. Cain brooded over his sense of being wronged, carefully planning what he would do. Both the man and the woman sought to avoid personal responsibility for what they had done by blaming another. Cain completely deflected any accountability by asking, "Am I my brother's keeper" (Genesis 4:9). In the story of the garden, the ground was cursed as part of the consequences of the man's act of disobedience. It produced thorns and thistles with which the man had to contend. In the story of Cain, Cain was cursed from the ground. The ground no longer yielded its strength (it abundance) to his efforts. In the story of the garden, the freedom and openness the couple enjoyed in relationship with the LORD God was replaced with fear, leading them to hide. The resulting relationship was marked with alienation from God. The story ended with the couple being ushered out of the garden. In the story of Cain, their alienation from the LORD God evolved into Cain's decision to move away from the presence of the LORD. He chose to live apart from the LORD. Cain's decision to have no relationship with the LORD resulted in Lamech, his great-great-great grandson, choosing to live out of a spirit of revenge expressed in unlimited, disproportionate retaliation. While Cain enjoyed the LORD's protection, Lamech chose to use violence as his protective shield, vowing to kill anyone who wronged him.

The story of Cain reflects how our choices never just impact us. They ripple out from us and down through the generations that follow us. This truth is expressly stated in the LORD's self-revelation to Moses on Mt. Sinai. After revealing the merciful and gracious nature of the divine character, the LORD added a clarifying word: "yet by no means clearing the guilty, but visiting the iniquity of the parents upon the children and the children's children, to the third and fourth generation" (Exodus 34:7b). The way the LORD dealt with sin—with mercy and compassion, by being slow to anger, with steadfast, faithful love, with forgiveness (Exodus 34:6—7a)—did not remove the consequences of sin. We experience the consequences of our choices, as the story of the garden reflects. And the consequences ripple through the generations that follow, as the story of Cain reflects. But there is good news in the midst of this sobering reality. In the Exodus 34 text, the consequences of sin extend to the third and fourth generations. The steadfast, faithful love of the LORD extends to the thousandth generation (Exodus 34:6). The contrast drawn between the third and fourth generation and the thousandth generation proclaims a great truth: the steadfast, faithful love of the LORD is greater than the consequences of our sins!

Am I My Brother's Keeper? (Genesis 4:9)

Living in relationship with others is an inescapable part of being human. While relationships enrich our lives immensely, they are also one of the most difficult dimensions of life. The story of Cain reflects our struggle with relationships. It simultaneously raises the issue of relationships in the family and relationships in society.

The struggle with relationships begins in our own families. The story of Cain reflects how siblings often view one another as rivals for their parent's attention, approval, and blessing. In the story of Cain, the LORD's regard for Abel's offering mirrors parental attention and approval. Like Cain in the story, older siblings often feel displaced by a younger sibling who comes along, consuming mother's attention and energies. The time, attention, and investment they once enjoyed are drained away by the arrival of the new brother/sister. On a deep, emotional level, the younger siblings become rivals, competitors, and, sometimes, adversaries.

Family relationships often take on a hierarchical tenor. The children in a family rarely enjoy an equal degree of standing, power, and voice. Their degree of standing, power, and voice is determined, to a large extent, by their birth order. Firstborns—whether a son or daughter—enjoy privilege that younger siblings do not. This privilege is seen in how younger siblings learn to defer to the firstborn. The privilege of the firstborn includes a greater position, standing, voice, and power within the family than those born after them. While this privileged or "blessed" status also involves responsibility, the responsibility is generally overshadowed by the position, standing, voice, and power the firstborn enjoys.[42] The privilege of the firstborn is different for girls who are firstborns than it is for sons who are firstborn. A firstborn son generally inherits a special position in the family's identity, even when they have a sister who was the firstborn. This special status is tied to their ability to carry on the family name. The specialness the firstborn son enjoys is often denied to the older, firstborn sister. The status of the firstborn is reflected in the contrast between the description of Cain's birth and that of Abel's (Genesis 4:1—2a).

The story of Cain also reflects the hierarchical rankings found in society. While all are created in the likeness of God, seldom are all viewed and valued equally. Some people enjoy greater standing, value, power, and voice than others. This greater standing is almost always associated with and accompanied by greater affluence, as well. Cain represents those who enjoy position and power, value and standing in society. Abel represents those who, lacking position and power, value and standing, are vulnerable to being exploited by those who have the power.

The story of Cain raises the question: what responsibility do those who enjoy position and power, value and standing, privilege and affluence have in relation to those who have none? This question captures a major theological struggle in the history of the people of Israel. It arises out of a central theological understanding in Israel.

Throughout Hebrew Scripture, the LORD (YWH) is portrayed as being the champion of the powerless and vulnerable while opposing the powerful and privileged who exploit them. This theological perspective is seen in the story of the Exodus in which LORD rescued the people of Israel from being slaves in Egypt. The LORD broke the power of Egypt, defeating its pantheon of gods in doing so, in order to set the people of Israel free from Egypt's domination and exploitation. Domination and exploitation—using power over another and against another for personal benefit—stand in contrast to the way the LORD uses power. As seen in the story of creation, God uses power to bring life into being and to nurture it into maturity. God uses power in life-giving, not life-depleting, ways.

This understanding of the LORD was a major theme in the preaching of the Hebrew prophets. The prophets repeatedly called the nation to use power on behalf of the powerless, particularly the widow, the orphan, the oppressed, and the alien. The technical term for this God-shaped way of using power was justice.[43] The long-awaited Messiah would bring peace by ruling with justice and righteousness. He would reject the world's way of using power over, down against another to control or destroy them. He would lead all nations to set aside the ways of war, the international expression of power used over, down against another.[44]

The psalmist praised the LORD for being a God who was the advocate of the powerless.

> Happy are those whose help is the God of Jacob,
> whose hope is in the LORD their God,

who made heaven and earth, the sea, and all that is in
them;
who keeps faith forever;
who executes justice *for the oppressed*;
who gives food to *the hungry*.
The LORD sets *the prisoners* free;
the LORD opens the eyes of *the blind*.
The LORD lifts up *those who are bowed down*;
the LORD loves the righteous.
The LORD watches over *the strangers*;
he upholds *the orphan and the widow*,
but the way of the wicked he brings to ruin (Psalm
146:5—9, emphasis added).

The two brothers in the story of Cain portray two classes of people:
the powerful and the powerless, the privileged and the poor, those
who have value and standing and those who have none, those with
voice and those with no voice. Cain is the firstborn whose birth is
celebrated as the work and gift of YWH. He occupies a place of special
importance and privilege in the family. His name suggests strength
and power. Abel's name, by contrast, suggests that which is powerless
and fleeting. It implies something insignificant that has no lasting
value. He holds a secondary position in the story, identified in relation
to Cain as "his brother Abel."

The story of Cain captures the struggle of the nation to live out
their understanding of justice. In the story, Cain's anger represents the
attitude of the powerful and privileged as they were called to use their
power on behalf of the powerless. Cain's question "Am I my brother's
keeper?" (Genesis 4:9) expresses the question of those who enjoyed
position and power, value and standing, privilege and affluence while
others suffered want. What responsibility do people of power, privilege,
and affluence have in relation to those who are powerless and poor?

This question lies at the heart of every group of people who seek
to live together in community, whether they live together as a church
or as a city or as a nation. It is a question that must be answered. It
cannot be ignored. How it is answered determines the character of that
community or nation.

The story of Cain prevents those who enjoyed privilege, power,
and affluence in the nation of Israel from ignoring the poor and

powerless. It is, for the nation, like the parable of the one sheep the prophet Nathan used to confront King David of his sin with Bathsheba (2 Samuel 12:1—15a). Nathan used the parable to help David see what he could not see. The story of Cain called the nation to wrestle with an issue they wanted to ignore. It is an issue with which we still struggle today.

So Cain Was Very Angry (Genesis 4:5)

Cain's reaction to the LORD's disregard of his offering was extreme. He was not just angry, but very angry. His disposition became dark and brooding (Genesis 4:5). The intensity of Cain's reaction suggests the experience touched him deeply, at the core of his being. So much so, he could not turn loose of it.

The story itself does not tell us the reason for Cain's reaction. It only describes the reaction. We are left to fill in the gap, based on our own experience. Again, part of the power of these stories is their ability to speak to our experiences. We identify with them.

In my commentary on Cain's anger (see again **Cain's Anger, Genesis 4:3—7** in Chapter 14), I attributed Cain's intense anger to him feeling displaced by Abel. The LORD had regard for Abel's offering while disregarding Cain's. In the LORD's response to the two offerings, Abel and his offering were valued while Cain and his offering were not. As the firstborn, Cain was accustomed to being valued over others. Cain's extreme reaction suggests that he personalized the LORD's disregard for his offering, interpreting it as a disregard of who he was. He felt devalued, losing the standing which he commonly enjoyed as the firstborn. At the same time, Abel gained value and standing. Abel took what Cain considered rightfully belonged to him.

This understanding of Cain's anger links Cain's sense of who he was with the status and standing, the power and privilege he enjoyed as the firstborn. His identity was wrapped up in the privilege of being the firstborn. As a result, the LORD's disregard for his offering struck at the very core of his identity. No wonder his emotional reaction was extreme! His sense of who he was had been undermined. The basis of his identity had been taken away. He lashed out in anger in order to protect what gave him his sense of value.

Again, the story captures a common human experience. How many of us have experienced intense emotional reactions whenever we have been disrespected, put down, or discounted?

Like Cain, many of us have been taught to link our sense of identity to something outside of ourselves. We tie our sense of who we are to a position we hold in the family (as Cain did) or in a group. We borrow value from our family heritage or from the school from which we graduated or from an organization to which we belong or from a company for which we work or from a political-moral-religious position we take. We have been trained to tie our sense of value to some kind of professional, academic, or economic accomplishment. We gain standing through our performance and our achievements.

Religious life provides another avenue for this kind of achievement-based identity. Every religious group defines what constitutes right belief, right behavior (morals), and proper worship. These norms of right belief, behavior, and worship become the standards by which we identify ourselves as "right" as well as the standards by which we judge others. These norms allow us to feel better than those who do not conform to them.

Achievement-based identities are merit-based identities. They are tied to what we have been able to do. Such identities always involve comparisons. We define ourselves over against others. "We are not like them. We don't do what they do." Judging others and criticizing what they do or don't do are natural products of (and evidence of!) our merit-based identities. Judging and criticizing allows us to unconsciously feel better than "those other people." Sometimes, when we fail to measure up to some standard of what is expected, achievement-based identities take on a negative tone marked by self-criticism, self-condemnation, and shame.

Cain's anger was directed at his brother Abel. Cain viewed his brother as a rival who had taken what was his. Cain viewed Abel as a competitor whom he had to defeat in order to win. He viewed his brother as an adversary he had to destroy.

How we view "the other" determines how we treat them. Our natural human response to those who are not like us is to focus on how they are different. How they are different makes us feel uncomfortable, stirring fear. As a result, we see those who are different through the eyes of fear. Seeing them through the eyes of fear leads us to view them as a rival that will take what is rightfully ours. Seeing through the eyes of fear, we view them as a threat that must be eliminated. When we view them through the eyes of fear, we naturally seek to protect ourselves by using our power against them. Cain saw Abel through the eyes of fear. As a result, he rose up against his brother and killed him (Genesis 4:8).

How we view the other is determined by how we view ourselves. This reality is reflected in the second part of what Jesus called the great commandment: "You shall love your neighbor *as yourself*" (Mark 12:31, emphasis added). When our sense of identity is based on something outside of ourselves—a position we hold, a group with which we are associated, something we accomplished—our sense of self, our sense of value will be fragile. We have to work to protect it and prop it up. Consequently, we view others as rivals, a threat to what we believe belongs to us.

In contrast, when our sense of identity is tied to God and God's love, claiming us as God's beloved children, then we no longer live out of fear. Our sense of identity along with our sense of value is secure. We are free to view and value, accept and embrace those who are different because we see them the way we see ourselves—as one made in the image of God and loved by God. We are free to love our neighbor because we live out of our identity as a beloved child of God, claimed by God's grace in Christ Jesus through the waters of baptism. The Spirit bears witness with our spirit that we are beloved children of God (Romans 8:14—17; Galatians 4:6—7).

This fear-based way of viewing and relating to others is the recurring story embedded in our human condition. It is the story of our personal relationships, including family relationships. It is the story of how different ethnic groups relate to one another. It is the story of why nations have gone to war with one another throughout human history. It is why the story of Cain speaks to us. How Cain viewed Abel, leading Cain to murder him, is how we view "the other."

Abel the Scapegoat

The way Cain avoided dealing with his anger was to target his brother Abel.

In the story of the garden, the couple avoided personal responsibility by blaming another. The man blamed the woman. The woman blamed the serpent. Cain took this pattern of avoiding-personal-responsibility-by-blaming to another level. Cain went beyond blaming Abel for his hurt. Cain made Abel the scapegoat.

Scapegoats are people—individuals or groups—that we identify as "the problem." If it were not for them, we believe, the problem would not exist. If we could eliminate them, the problem would go away and things would be better—at least for us![45]

Scapegoats are always people we view as "other." They are generally (but not always) someone or some group that is in a one-down position in relation to us. They are normally more vulnerable than us and enjoy less power than us.[46]

Scapegoating another allows us to feel "better than" than the other. It allows us to hold to the belief that "our way" is right and their way is wrong. In doing so, it blinds us to ourselves and our contribution to the problem. It allows us to escape any responsibility for finding a solution to the problem. By blaming the "other," we place the responsibility for the problem totally on the other. The responsibility for addressing and resolving the problem lies with them.

We all have scapegoats. Our scapegoat is the one we criticize, find fault with, and complain about.

Why Are You Angry? (Genesis 4:6)

The LORD questioned Cain about his anger. His question did not condemn Cain for his anger. It was an attempt to help Cain deal with his anger. It was an attempt to protect Cain from what he might do in his anger.

The LORD's question called Cain to be aware of the anger he was experiencing. More, it called him to see beyond the anger he felt to the source of the anger. It called him to learn from the anger, hearing what it said. The LORD called Cain to practice self-reflection and exercise self-awareness.

Self-reflection is what the term states: reflecting on ourselves and what we experienced. It is taking time to notice and reflect on our experiences—both the event and our reaction to it. The practice of self-reflection is rooted in the willingness to learn about ourselves in the pursuit of growth and greater maturity.

Self-awareness is awareness of what we are experiencing on a semi-conscious or unconscious level *as an incident is taking place*. It is awareness that moves us beyond the surface of our lives to the interior realm of our lives. Self-awareness is a skill we develop as we practice self-reflection.

Self-awareness allows us to move beyond the emotional reactivity of the moment. It allows us to think clearly about what we have experienced, how we interpret it, and what we will do in response to it.

Self-awareness positions us to exercise self-control. Apart from self-awareness, we react in automatic, unconscious, self-protective ways. Self-control or self-management is what allows us to move beyond these old, preconditioned, emotionally immature ways of reacting. It allows us to consciously choose how we will respond (as opposed to react).

Self-reflection, self-awareness, and self-control are essential skills on the spiritual journey. They are how we grow emotionally-relationally-spiritually.[47] In questioning Cain about his anger, the LORD was inviting him to practice self-reflection. The LORD was guiding him away from a path that led to sin onto a path that led to emotional-relational-spiritual progress.

When we do not live with self-awareness, we automatically get stuck in our feelings—just as Cain did. We become consumed with and dwell on what we are feeling—just as Cain brooded on his pain and coddled his anger. Our feelings take over, dictating what we do—just as Cain's harbored anger led him to murder his brother Abel.

Life is full of painful experiences. Every such experience is an opportunity to learn about ourselves … when we practice self-reflection and self-awareness. Self-reflection leading to self-awareness positions us to exercise self-control, allowing us to grow and change. Self-reflection, self-awareness, and self-control empower us to function in more mature, healthier ways. Our challenge in such situations is to move beyond being emotionally reactive. It is to move beyond our natural tendency to blame others the way the couple did in the story of the garden and to attack others the way Cain attacked his brother Abel.

Living in the Land of Nod (Genesis 4:16)

The land of Nod in which Cain settled refers to an emotional-spiritual condition rather than to a physical location. (As noted above, the Hebrew word translated as Nod means restless.) The condition is one we can experience anywhere and everywhere.

The reference to Cain living in the land of Nod is a description of his life after he killed his brother Abel. An inner restless marked his life. He lived with a deep-seated dis-ease in the core of his being. A nebulous sense of anxiety haunted his inner thoughts and dominated his waking hours. It was as though he was always looking over his shoulder in fear of something that was stalking him even though he could not give that something a name. Inner peace was something he never knew.

This inner restlessness manifested itself outwardly in the way he lived. He lived as a fugitive and a wanderer (Genesis 4:14). He had no place where he was at home. There was no place where he felt he belonged, where he felt accepted, where he felt valued, where he felt safe. He sought to quiet the inner restlessness by filling his life with physical things. But nothing satisfied him. He did not know how to be content. He was always on the move, looking for the next whatever, hoping against hope that—maybe, just maybe—the next thing would fill the hollow void in his heart.

The condition of our inner life is inseparably tied to our relationship with God. We experience inner peace as we learn to rest in God's steadfast, faithful love. We know what it is to be content as we learn to trust God's generosity and unfailing provision. We find what it means to be at home—to be accepted, to be valued, to be safe, to be loved—as we live in faithful obedience to the LORD.

Cain's restless condition was the natural result of his decision to go away from the presence of God (Genesis 4:16).

The LORD's Mark on Cain (Genesis 4:15b)

In the story of the garden, the nature of the LORD God was reflected in what God did. The nature of the LORD is also seen in the story of Cain in how the LORD related to Cain.

Eve identified the LORD's role in Cain's birth (Genesis 4:1). Cain was conceived and born through the LORD's help.

The LORD lived in relationship with Cain and his brother Abel, receiving their gifts and offerings (Genesis 4:3-4).

The LORD had regard for Abel and his offering but not for Cain and his offering (Genesis 4:4b—5). Again, the story does not give an explanation for how the LORD responded to each of them.

The LORD questioned Cain when he was angry and brooding on his pain in his self-absorbed focus (Genesis 4:6—7). The confrontation was an attempt to protect Cain from the possible sin that was lurking like a wild animal, waiting to pounce on him. It was an attempt to encourage him to deal with his feelings so that he would not be controlled by them. It was an attempt to steer Cain away from the path of self-destruction.

The LORD questioned Cain again after he had killed his brother Abel (Genesis 4:9). This confrontation offered Cain the opportunity to deal honestly with what he had done. It gave Cain the opportunity to own the responsibility for his actions. A wrong can only be addressed through honesty that owns personal responsibility. The theological term for such honesty is confession. The honesty of confession does not right the wrong, but it opens the door to the possibility of resolution and reconciliation. The witness of scripture is that the LORD responds to our wrongdoing with forgiveness. We access that forgiveness through confession—honesty that owns responsibility for our actions.

The LORD refused to allow Cain to avoid the reality of what he had done (Genesis 4:10). Abel's death at Cain's hand called for accountability. We never "get away with" the wrong we have done. The gift of the LORD's forgiveness gives us the courage to face our choices.

The LORD gave Cain what he chose, the consequences of his actions (Genesis 4:11—12), just as the LORD God did with the man and the woman in the story of the garden (Genesis 3:14—19). The consequences were Cain's punishment for what he had done.

The LORD did not abandon Cain as he experienced the consequences of his murder of Abel. The LORD put a mark on Cain to protect him from those who would harm or kill him. To reinforce that protection, the LORD promised divine (seven-fold) retribution on any who harmed Cain (Genesis 4:15).

The story of Cain reflects the steadfast love of the LORD that refuses to give up on us or abandon us. It tells the story of the LORD's faithfulness in the face of our inability to be faithful. It is the story of the nation of Israel. It is our story.

A Guide for Personal Reflection and Journaling, for Group Conversation and Discussion

1. What is your reaction to the concept of the ripple effect of sin? How have you experienced it in your own life? Where have you seen its impact ripple outward into the lives of others, particularly the next generations? Where have you seen the steadfast love of God overcome the ripple effects of sin, either in your life or in the life of another?

2. What is your reaction to the interpretation that the Cain-Abel story represents two classes of people: the powerful and the powerless? With which group do you identify? Why?

3. What is your reaction to the concept that God advocates for the powerless and calls God's people to do so, too? How does that understanding play out in your life and relationships? How does it play out in the life of your church or spiritual community?

4. Identify a time in your life when you have felt displaced. What reactions stirred inside you in the experience? What was your attitude toward the one who caused the displacement? How did you resolve it?

5. What things outside of yourself do you use to create your identity and validate your value? When has your sense of identity (value) been threatened?

6. Who is someone you view through the lens of fear? How does your fear color your perception of them? What about them do you fear?

7. Who—what individual or group—do you use as a scapegoat? Hint: who do you criticize and blame? What about them do you dislike? What do they represent to you? What about yourself are you avoiding by focusing on them?

8. Identify how self-reflection, self-awareness, and self-control are a part of your life. What impact have these emotional-relational-spiritual skills had in your life, spiritually and relationally?

9. When have you experienced the inner restlessness of the land of Nod? How do you attempt to "still" this inner restlessness? What do you do to access the peace of God?

10. What does the story of Cain teach you about the LORD?

FROM ADAM TO NOAH: A GENEALOGICAL BRIDGE

Genesis 5:1—32

Genesis 5:1—32

This is the list of the descendants of Adam. When God created humankind, he made them in the likeness of God. ²Male and female he created them, and he blessed them and named them "Humankind" when they were created.

³When Adam had lived one hundred thirty years, he became the father of a son in his likeness, according to his image, and named him Seth. ⁴The days of Adam after he became the father of Seth were eight hundred years; and he had other sons and daughters. ⁵Thus all the days that Adam lived were nine hundred thirty years; and he died.

⁶When Seth had lived one hundred five years, he became the father of Enosh. ⁷Seth lived after the birth of Enosh eight hundred seven years, and had other sons and daughters. ⁸Thus all the days of Seth were nine hundred twelve years; and he died.

⁹When Enosh had lived ninety years, he became the father of Kenan. ¹⁰Enosh lived after the birth of Kenan eight hundred fifteen years, and had other sons and daughters. ¹¹Thus all the days of Enosh were nine hundred five years; and he died.

¹²When Kenan had lived seventy years, he became the father of Mahalalel. ¹³Kenan lived after the birth of Mahalalel eight hundred and forty years, and had other sons and daughters. ¹⁴Thus all the days of Kenan were nine hundred and ten years; and he died.

¹⁵When Mahalalel had lived sixty-five years, he became the father of Jared. ¹⁶Mahalalel lived after the birth of Jared eight hundred thirty years, and had other sons and daughters. ¹⁷Thus all the days of Mahalalel were eight hundred ninety-five years; and he died.

¹⁸When Jared had lived one hundred sixty-two years he became the father of Enoch. ¹⁹Jared lived after the birth of Enoch eight hundred years, and had other sons and daughters. ²⁰Thus all the days of Jared were nine hundred sixty-two years; and he died.

²¹When Enoch had lived sixty-five years, he became the father of Methuselah. ²²Enoch walked with God after the birth of Methuselah three hundred years, and had other sons and daughters. ²³Thus all the days of Enoch were three hundred sixty-five years. ²⁴Enoch walked with God; then he was no more, because God took him.

²⁵When Methuselah had lived one hundred eighty-seven years, he became the father of Lamech. ²⁶Methuselah lived after the birth of Lamech seven hundred eighty-two years, and had other sons and

daughters. [27]Thus all the days of Methuselah were nine hundred sixty-nine years; and he died.

[28]When Lamech had lived one hundred eighty-two years, he became the father of a son; [29]he named him Noah, saying, "Out of the ground that the LORD has cursed this one shall bring us relief from our work and from the toil of our hands." [30]Lamech lived after the birth of Noah five hundred ninety-five years, and had other sons and daughters. [31]Thus all the days of Lamech were seven hundred seventy-seven years; and he died. [32]After Noah was five hundred years old, Noah became the father of Shem, Ham, and Japheth.

CHAPTER 16

GENEALOGY: THE STORY
WITHIN THE STORY

The editor of Genesis used three genealogical tables to link the five stories together. This first table links the story of the garden with the story of Noah and the flood. The genealogies are more than bridges between the stories. They advance the stories. Even more, they tell a story in and of themselves.

The account of the birth of Seth (Genesis 4:25—26) set the stage for the genealogy of Adam. Adam's descendants were traced through Seth, not Cain, even though Cain was the firstborn. Seth was chosen because his line walked in intentional relationship with the LORD. These early stories are the prelude to the story of the people of Israel who lived in covenant relationship with the LORD. They viewed them as a part of their history. As we saw in the story of the garden, they also viewed them as a reflection of their history. The stories of Seth's descendants are how they as the people of God, during and after the exile, understood they were to live—walking with God in faithful obedience. The story of Cain and his descendants were a reminder of how they didn't want to live. Cain's story served as a strong warning about what happens when they walked away from the LORD rather than walking with the LORD.

The genealogy begins with the editor's note indicating a shift in the story: "this is the list of the descendants of Adam" (Genesis 5:1). Ten different times the editor used the phrase "these are the generations of" to indicate a progression in the story line.[48]

The account of the birth of Seth (Genesis 4:25—26) uses the name "the LORD" to refer to God. The genealogy of Adam does not use this covenant name. It simply speaks of "God." The genealogy is from a different tradition than the stories of the garden and of Cain (which includes the account of the birth of Seth).

The genealogy follows a repeated pattern: the age at which the ancestor became the father of his firstborn along with the name of his firstborn, the number of years the ancestor lived after the birth of his firstborn during which he became the father of other sons and daughters, the total number of years the ancestor lived, and his death. This pattern is disrupted three times. The disruption calls attention to those particular descendants. The disruptions are found in the second, seventh and ninth generations. The second generation is Seth; the seventh generation is Enoch; the ninth is Lamech, the father of Noah.

One of the first things in the genealogy that strikes the modern reader is the ages that are recorded. Adam and all but three of his descendants lived to be over nine hundred years old. Mahalelel fell short of nine hundred by five years. Enoch was taken by God at the age of three hundred sixty-five years. Lamech, the father of Noah, lived to be seven hundred seventy-seven years old. Such extreme longevity (in our minds) raises questions about the historical accuracy of these ages. Did people really live to be that old during that time? Did they count years the way we today count years? How do we explain such longevity?

These kinds of questions are products of our scientifically-oriented thinking which looks for facts to believe.[49] Although we want answers to our questions, the text does not answer them. We are given a choice. We can speculate about what the answers might be, knowing our speculation takes us away from the text and what the text intended to communicate, or we can set our questions and speculation aside so we can give our attention to identifying the truth the story conveys.

We will see in the introduction to the story of Noah and the flood that, after this genealogy, the LORD placed a limit on how long humans would live (Genesis 6:3). The next genealogy listed (Genesis 10:1—32) does not include ages. In the third genealogy, the longevity of the descendants is greatly reduced, ranging from two hundred to six hundred years. The ages of Abraham and his descendants range from one hundred to two hundred years old.

This genealogy identifies ten generations from Adam to Noah. Ancient Babylon also had a story of a universal flood that was preceded by a genealogy of ten generations. The story of a flood that destroyed the world was not unique to Israel. How the story was used by the editor of Genesis is its unique feature for the people of Israel.

Adam's genealogy begins with God, not Adam (Genesis 5:1—2). It reaches back beyond the story of the garden to the story of creation when God created humankind in the divine likeness (Genesis 1:26). This opening statement in Adam's genealogy tied the story of creation to the story of the garden. It applied the creation of humankind in the divine likeness to the man Adam from the story of the garden. In this reference, the editor of Genesis harmonized the two stories. These verses also tied the story of the nation of Israel back to God's creation of the world.

Just as Adam was created "in the likeness of God," so his son Seth was said to be "in his likeness, according to his image" (Genesis 5:3). The wording duplicates Genesis 1:26 in which humankind was created in the likeness and image of God. As Adam was made in God's likeness, so Seth was made in Adam's likeness. Seth, thereby, was also made in God's likeness. He, like Adam, was a son of God. As descendants of Adam and Seth, the people of Israel saw themselves as having been created in the likeness and image of God. They were created to live the ways of God by walking with God in faithful obedience.

As in Cain's genealogy, the seventh generation is important in Seth's genealogy. In this seventh generation, the repeated patterned of the genealogical table is interrupted. The interruption calls our attention to the meaning reflected in it. Two different times the text tells us "Enoch walked with God" (Genesis 5:22, 24). The phrase "walked with God" brings to mind the story of the garden where the LORD God walked with the man and woman, enjoying the cool breeze of the evening (Genesis 3:8). It carries the idea of personal fellowship with God. Enoch walked with God as Adam walked with the LORD God in the garden. Enoch as the seventh generation stands in contrast to Lamech who was the seventh generation in Cain's line. While Enoch walked in relationship with God, Lamech had no need of God or God's protection. He would avenge himself. Enoch was a model for the nation of Israel. They, too, were to walk with God in faithful obedience.

Enoch's genealogical reference ends differently from that of the other generations. The pattern ends each record with the words "and he died." But Enoch's record has no reference to his death. Instead, the text noted "then he was no more, because God took him" (Genesis 5:24). Life after the garden included the experience of death, but Enoch did not experience death. His experience of escaping death was said to be the work of God: "because God took him." It was tied to his walk with God. The only other person in Hebrew scripture to not experience death was the prophet Elijah. He was taken by a chariot of fire, ascending into heaven in a whirlwind (2 Kings 2:11). The LORD took him.

The people of Israel in exile would have understood this reference to Enoch in light of their exile experience. Had they walked in faithful obedience to the LORD, they would have avoided death, i.e., their experience of the death of their nation and exile in Babylon. They would have seen Enoch as the model for how they were to live. They, like Enoch, were to walk with God in faithful obedience.

Death is one of the things we humans fear the most. It confronts us with our ultimate experience of powerlessness. It threatens us with the loss of everything we have known and valued, including our very self. It thrusts us into the great unknown. The only resource we have available in facing it is faith—faith in God's steadfast, faithful love that does not abandon us, faith that death is not the end, faith that death, like birth, is a transition to life in another dimension of reality. Such faith is strengthened by the story of Jesus's death and resurrection. God raised Jesus from the dead, defeating, transcending, and transforming death. The Apostle Paul called him "the first fruits of those who have died" (1 Corinthians 15:20). His resurrection holds forth the hope that death is not everything we fear it to be. While death continues to be a part of our human experience, the resurrection of Jesus transforms it for us. Paul spoke of death as "the last enemy to be destroyed" (1 Corinthians 15:26). Unlike Enoch, we will experience the reality of death. We face this reality with faith, confident in the hope of the resurrection. Although we will be unlike Enoch, we shall be like Christ. Such is the Christian hope.

Adam's genealogy ends with Noah, the tenth generation. Noah was the target of the genealogical table just as Lamech was the target of Cain's genealogical table. The disruption of the repeated pattern in the genealogy focuses on the hope associated with his birth. His father—also named Lamech—expressed the hope for relief from the way things were. He expressed hope for a new beginning—a restart. Lamech chose a name for his son that reflected this desire for relief. The name Noah means "rest, comfort, peace." The relief for which Lamech longed was relief from the curse on the ground that made work toilsome and hard.

The reference to "the ground that the LORD has cursed" linked the story of Noah and the flood to the story of the garden.

The longing expressed by Lamech at Noah's birth is a common part of our human condition. We often long for relief from the way things are. We long for a new beginning that offers the prospect that things can be different, better.

Because of this longing, we often look for a savior—someone who will help us escape our current reality, someone who will bring about a new and better reality. Lamech viewed his son as a savior. "Out of the ground that the LORD has cursed this one shall bring us relief from our work and from the toil of our hands" (Genesis 5:29).

Our desire to escape a painful situation often overlooks the underlying problem. The curse of the ground was one of the consequences of the couple's choice to live out of their own will, following their own wisdom, rather than in faithful obedience to the LORD. The core problem was the self-reliant, self-serving spirit out of which they made their choice. The problem was what was in the human heart. This inner problem is expressly stated in the introduction to the story of Noah and the flood: "The LORD saw that the wickedness of humankind was great in the earth, and that *every inclination of the thoughts of their hearts was only evil* continually" (Genesis 6:5, emphasis added).

The prophet Jeremiah emphasized the heart as the source of sin:

> The sin of Judah is written with an iron pen;
> with a diamond point it is engraved on the table of
> their hearts" (Jeremiah 17:1),

and

> The heart is devious above all else;
> it is perverse—
> who can understand it?
> I the LORD test the mind
> and search the heart" (Jeremiah 17:9—10a).

Jesus also pointed to this inner reality:

> For it is from within, *from the human heart,* that evil
> intentions come: fornication, theft, murder, adultery,
> avarice, wickedness, deceit, licentiousness, envy,

slander, pride, folly. All these evil things come *from within* (Mark 7:21—23, emphasis added).

The Apostle Paul spoke of being a slave to sin—"sold into slavery under sin" (Romans 7:14)—to describe this inner reality. Paul drew a contrast between sin as a principle to which he was enslaved and sin as doing what he did not want to do (Romans 7:7—25). This distinction can be expressed by talking about Sin (with a capital S) and sins (plural). Sin (with a capital S) is the disease; sins (plural) are the symptoms. Sin (with a capital S) is the root; sins (plural) are the fruit. Sin (with a capital S) is the self-reliant, self-serving spirit; sins (plural) are the acts of disobedience (behavior). We can only eliminate the sins (plural—the symptoms, the fruit, the behavior) by dealing with the Sin (the disease, the root, the self-reliant, self-serving spirit). While we can, through self-effort, change our behavior, we are powerless to change what is in our hearts. The attitudes and spirit out of which we live are not subject to the power of our will. We need a savior to deliver us from what is in our hearts. Such is the work of the Spirit (Romans 8:1—17) and the essence of the spiritual journey.

We will see in the story of Noah and the flood that the relief for which Lamech longed came through God's covenant relationship with us as humans.

A Guide for Personal Reflection and Journaling, for Group Conversation and Discussion

1. What new thought or understanding did you gain from this interpretation of the genealogy?
2. The interpretation of the genealogy raises the issue of death. How do you view death? How do you deal with the concept of death? What do you experience when you think about your own death?
3. When have you experienced the desire for relief that Lamech voiced? When have you wanted a new beginning? How did you deal with that desire?
4. What is your reaction to the emphasis upon the inner realm of the heart? What is one way your heart been changed on your spiritual journey?

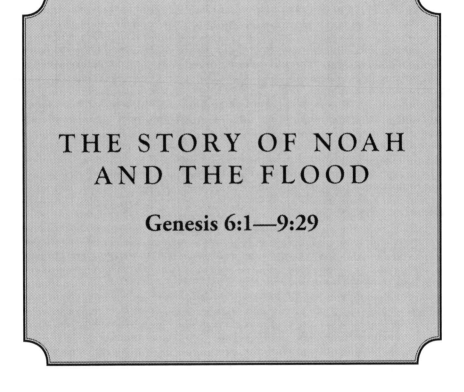

THE STORY OF NOAH
AND THE FLOOD

Genesis 6:1—9:29

Genesis 6:1—9:29

Genesis 6—When people began to multiply on the face of the ground, and daughters were born to them, ²the sons of God saw that they were fair; and they took wives for themselves of all that they chose. ³Then the LORD said, "My spirit shall not abide in mortals forever, for they are flesh; their days shall be one hundred twenty years." ⁴The Nephilim were on the earth in those days—and also afterward—when the sons of God went in to the daughters of humans, who bore children to them. These were the heroes that were of old, warriors of renown.

⁵The LORD saw that the wickedness of humankind was great in the earth, and that every inclination of the thoughts of their hearts was only evil continually. ⁶And the LORD was sorry that he had made humankind on the earth, and it grieved him to his heart. ⁷So the LORD said, "I will blot out from the earth the human beings I have created—people together with animals and creeping things and birds of the air, for I am sorry that I have made them." ⁸But Noah found favor in the sight of the LORD.

⁹These are the descendants of Noah. Noah was a righteous man, blameless in his generation; Noah walked with God. ¹⁰And Noah had three sons, Shem, Ham, and Japheth.

¹¹Now the earth was corrupt in God's sight, and the earth was filled with violence. ¹²And God saw that the earth was corrupt; for all flesh had corrupted its ways upon the earth. ¹³And God said to Noah, "I have determined to make an end of all flesh, for the earth is filled with violence because of them; now I am going to destroy them along with the earth. ¹⁴Make yourself an ark of cypress wood; make rooms in the ark, and cover it inside and out with pitch. ¹⁵This is how you are to make it: the length of the ark three hundred cubits, its width fifty cubits, and its height thirty cubits. ¹⁶Make a roof for the ark, and finish it to a cubit above; and put the door of the ark in its side; make it with lower, second, and third decks. ¹⁷For my part, I am going to bring a flood of waters on the earth, to destroy from under heaven all flesh in which is the breath of life; everything that is on the earth shall die. ¹⁸But I will establish my covenant with you; and you shall come into the ark, you, your sons, your wife, and your sons' wives with you. ¹⁹And of every living thing, of all flesh, you shall bring two of every kind into the ark, to keep them alive with you; they shall be male and female.

²⁰Of the birds according to their kinds, and of the animals according to their kinds, of every creeping thing of the ground according to its kind, two of every kind shall come in to you, to keep them alive. ²¹Also take with you every kind of food that is eaten, and store it up; and it shall serve as food for you and for them." ²²Noah did this; he did all that God commanded him.

Genesis 7—Then the LORD said to Noah, "Go into the ark, you and all your household, for I have seen that you alone are righteous before me in this generation. ²Take with you seven pairs of all clean animals, the male and its mate; and a pair of the animals that are not clean, the male and its mate; ³and seven pairs of the birds of the air also, male and female, to keep their kind alive on the face of all the earth. ⁴For in seven days I will send rain on the earth for forty days and forty nights; and every living thing that I have made I will blot out from the face of the ground."

⁵And Noah did all that the LORD had commanded him. ⁶Noah was six hundred years old when the flood of waters came on the earth. ⁷And Noah with his sons and his wife and his sons' wives went into the ark to escape the waters of the flood. ⁸Of clean animals, and of animals that are not clean, and of birds, and of everything that creeps on the ground, ⁹two and two, male and female, went into the ark with Noah, as God had commanded Noah. ¹⁰And after seven days the waters of the flood came on the earth.

¹¹In the six hundredth year of Noah's life, in the second month, on the seventeenth day of the month, on that day all the fountains of the great deep burst forth, and the windows of the heavens were opened. ¹²The rain fell on the earth forty days and forty nights. ¹³On the very same day Noah with his sons, Shem and Ham and Japheth, and Noah's wife and the three wives of his sons entered the ark, ¹⁴they and every wild animal of every kind, and all domestic animals of every kind, and every creeping thing that creeps on the earth, and every bird of every kind—every bird, every winged creature. ¹⁵They went into the ark with Noah, two and two of all flesh in which there was the breath of life. ¹⁶And those that entered, male and female of all flesh, went in as God had commanded him; and the LORD shut him in.

¹⁷The flood continued forty days on the earth; and the waters increased, and bore up the ark, and it rose high above the earth. ¹⁸The waters swelled and increased greatly on the earth; and the ark floated

on the face of the waters. ¹⁹The waters swelled so mightily on the earth that all the high mountains under the whole heaven were covered; ²⁰the waters swelled above the mountains, covering them fifteen cubits deep. ²¹And all flesh died that moved on the earth, birds, domestic animals, wild animals, all swarming creatures that swarm on the earth, and all human beings; ²²everything on dry land in whose nostrils was the breath of life died. ²³He blotted out every living thing that was on the face of the ground, human beings and animals and creeping things and birds of the air; they were blotted out from the earth. Only Noah was left, and those that were with him in the ark. ²⁴And the waters swelled on the earth for one hundred fifty days.

Genesis 8—But God remembered Noah and all the wild animals and all the domestic animals that were with him in the ark. And God made a wind blow over the earth, and the waters subsided; ²the fountains of the deep and the windows of the heavens were closed, the rain from the heavens was restrained, ³and the waters gradually receded from the earth. At the end of one hundred fifty days the waters had abated; ⁴and in the seventh month, on the seventeenth day of the month, the ark came to rest on the mountains of Ararat. ⁵The waters continued to abate until the tenth month; in the tenth month, on the first day of the month, the tops of the mountains appeared.

⁶At the end of forty days Noah opened the window of the ark that he had made ⁷and sent out the raven; and it went to and fro until the waters were dried up from the earth. ⁸Then he sent out the dove from him, to see if the waters had subsided from the face of the ground; ⁹but the dove found no place to set its foot, and it returned to him to the ark, for the waters were still on the face of the whole earth. So he put out his hand and took it and brought it into the ark with him. ¹⁰He waited another seven days, and again he sent out the dove from the ark; ¹¹and the dove came back to him in the evening, and there in its beak was a freshly plucked olive leaf; so Noah knew that the waters had subsided from the earth. ¹²Then he waited another seven days, and sent out the dove; and it did not return to him any more.

¹³In the six hundred first year, in the first month, the first day of the month, the waters were dried up from the earth; and Noah removed the covering of the ark, and looked, and saw that the face of the ground was drying. ¹⁴In the second month, on the twenty-seventh day of the month, the earth was dry. ¹⁵Then God said to Noah, ¹⁶"Go

out of the ark, you and your wife, and your sons and your sons' wives with you. ¹⁷Bring out with you every living thing that is with you of all flesh—birds and animals and every creeping thing that creeps on the earth—so that they may abound on the earth, and be fruitful and multiply on the earth." ¹⁸So Noah went out with his sons and his wife and his sons' wives. ¹⁹And every animal, every creeping thing, and every bird, everything that moves on the earth, went out of the ark by families.

²⁰Then Noah built an altar to the LORD, and took of every clean animal and of every clean bird, and offered burnt offerings on the altar. ²¹And when the LORD smelled the pleasing odor, the LORD said in his heart, "I will never again curse the ground because of humankind, for the inclination of the human heart is evil from youth; nor will I ever again destroy every living creature as I have done. ²²As long as the earth endures, seedtime and harvest, cold and heat, summer and winter, day and night, shall not cease."

Genesis 9—God blessed Noah and his sons, and said to them, "Be fruitful and multiply, and fill the earth. ²The fear and dread of you shall rest on every animal of the earth, and on every bird of the air, on everything that creeps on the ground, and on all the fish of the sea; into your hand they are delivered. ³Every moving thing that lives shall be food for you; and just as I gave you the green plants, I give you everything. ⁴Only, you shall not eat flesh with its life, that is, its blood. ⁵For your own lifeblood I will surely require a reckoning: from every animal I will require it and from human beings, each one for the blood of another, I will require a reckoning for human life.

⁶Whoever sheds the blood of a human,

by a human shall that person's blood be shed;

for in his own image God made humankind.

⁷And you, be fruitful and multiply, abound on the earth and multiply in it."

⁸Then God said to Noah and to his sons with him, ⁹"As for me, I am establishing my covenant with you and your descendants after you, ¹⁰and with every living creature that is with you, the birds, the domestic animals, and every animal of the earth with you, as many as came out of the ark. ¹¹I establish my covenant with you, that never again shall all flesh be cut off by the waters of a flood, and never again shall there be a flood to destroy the earth."

¹²God said, "This is the sign of the covenant that I make between me and you and every living creature that is with you, for all future generations: ¹³I have set my bow in the clouds, and it shall be a sign of the covenant between me and the earth. ¹⁴When I bring clouds over the earth and the bow is seen in the clouds, ¹⁵I will remember my covenant that is between me and you and every living creature of all flesh; and the waters shall never again become a flood to destroy all flesh. ¹⁶When the bow is in the clouds, I will see it and remember the everlasting covenant between God and every living creature of all flesh that is on the earth." ¹⁷God said to Noah, "This is the sign of the covenant that I have established between me and all flesh that is on the earth."

¹⁸The sons of Noah who went out of the ark were Shem, Ham, and Japheth. Ham was the father of Canaan. ¹⁹These three were the sons of Noah; and from these the whole earth was peopled.

²⁰Noah, a man of the soil, was the first to plant a vineyard. ²¹He drank some of the wine and became drunk, and he lay uncovered in his tent. ²²And Ham, the father of Canaan, saw the nakedness of his father, and told his two brothers outside. ²³Then Shem and Japheth took a garment, laid it on both their shoulders, and walked backward and covered the nakedness of their father; their faces were turned away, and they did not see their father's nakedness.

²⁴When Noah awoke from his wine and knew what his youngest son had done to him, ²⁵he said,

"Cursed be Canaan; lowest of slaves shall he be to his brothers."
²⁶He also said,
"Blessed by the LORD my God be Shem;
and let Canaan be his slave.
²⁷May God make space for Japheth,
and let him live in the tents of Shem;
and let Canaan be his slave."

²⁸After the flood Noah lived three hundred fifty years. ²⁹All the days of Noah were nine hundred fifty years; and he died.

CHAPTER 17

INTRODUCING THE STORY OF
NOAH AND THE FLOOD

T he story of Noah and the flood is not unique to the Hebrew
Scriptures. Similar stories are found in many ancient cultures.
As was mentioned in the previous chapter, the nation of Babylon had
a flood story that was preceded by a ten generation genealogical table.
While the Hebrew account of the flood is not unique, it has unique
features that set it apart from other accounts.

Two in One

The biblical account is a combination of two different accounts
woven together. Each of the two accounts came from a different source
within the nation's history. One came from what is known as the E
source. This version used the name God (*Elohim*) to speak of God. The
other version used the name the LORD (YWH) to speak of God. It is
known as the J (for the word YWH) source. It is associated with the
southern kingdom of Judah.

These two accounts were woven together, creating a duplication
and repetition of different parts of the story. The interwoven accounts
also result in different and sometimes conflicting details.

The decision to destroy the earth is first told from the J source,
followed by an account from the E source. The E version of entering
the ark is found in Genesis 7:6—12; Genesis 7:11—24 is the J version.
(Note the use of the name the LORD in verse 16.) The two versions

each offer an explanation of the covenant God made with creation following the flood. Genesis 8:20—22 is the J version; Genesis 9:1—17 is the E version.

In addition to these duplications, the interweaving of these two different versions produced a conflict in the details of the story. In the E version, Noah was instructed to take two of every living thing, Genesis 6:19—20. In the J version, the LORD's instructions were to take seven pairs of animals that were designated as clean and one pair of animals that were considered unclean, Genesis 7:1—3. The distinction between clean and unclean animals suggests the original version was adapted by the J source after the clean-unclean designation was established. This distinction reflects the interests of the southern kingdom of Judah where worship at the Temple was central. The clean-unclean designation was created to identify eligibility for worship in the Temple.

The Language and Imagery of the Story

The story of Noah and the flood is tied to and told against the backdrop of the story of creation and the story of the garden. Language and imagery from the two previous stories are embedded in the flood story. This language and imagery make the biblical account of the flood significantly different from the accounts found in other cultures.

In the story of creation, the phrase "and God saw," (Genesis 1:4, etc.) was used on each of the first six days of creation. This same phrase surfaces early in the flood story, Genesis 6:5, 12. In the story of creation, what God saw was good, then very good. In the flood story, what God saw was the opposite of good: the earth was corrupt. In the story of creation, the phrase "and God said" was also used on each of the six days of creation (Genesis 1:3, etc.). It too is used early in the flood story, Genesis 6:7, 13. In the story of creation, what God said brought creation into being. In the flood story, what God said warned of the coming destruction of creation.

On the second day in the story of creation, God established a dome in the midst of the waters, separating the waters below the dome from those above it (Genesis 1:6—7). In the flood story, those two waters converged to reverse that original creative process. The fountains or springs of the earth burst forth, joining the rain from the sky—"the windows of the heavens"—to return creation to its original state when the waters of chaos covered the face of the earth (Genesis 1:2).

> And the waters increased ... The waters swelled and increased greatly on the earth ... The waters swelled so mightily on the earth that all the high mountains under the whole heaven were covered; the waters swelled above the mountains (Genesis 7:17, 18, 19, 20).

The flood story describes the return to chaos.

In the story of creation, God filled the sky with birds, the sea with fish, and the land with cattle, creeping things, and the wild animals (Genesis 1:20—21, 24—25). The flood destroyed every living thing on the land that was named in the creation story, leaving the world empty and in need of being repopulated (Genesis 7:21—23). Everything "in whose nostrils was the breath of life died" (Genesis 7:22). The reference reverses the LORD God's creation of the man from the dust of the earth, breathing "into his nostrils the breath of life; and the man became a living being" (Genesis 2:7).

In the story of creation, the wind of God swept across the face of the watery chaos as God began to call creation into being (Genesis 1:2). The waters of the flood began to recede when "God made a wind blow over the earth" (Genesis 8:1).

After Noah, his sons, and the animals left the ark, God blessed them and commanded them "Be fruitful and multiply, and fill the earth" (Genesis 9:1, see also Genesis 8:17 and 9:7). This was the same command God gave in the creation story (Genesis 1:22, 28).

Finally, in the covenant God made following the flood, the LORD swore to never again curse the ground (Genesis 8:21). The curse of the ground was one of the consequences of the couple's act of disobedience in the story of the garden (Genesis 3:17).

The Sons of God and the Daughters of Men, Genesis 6:1—4

Sandwiched between Adam's genealogical table and the story of Noah and the flood are four verses that have created questions for anyone who tries to understand them. The verses are some of the oldest material found in the Hebrew Scriptures. Some of the words in the original material and their meaning are difficult to understand.

The verses describe the intermarriage between the sons of God and the daughters of men (Genesis 6:1—2). This intermarrying apparently produced the Nephilim (Genesis 6:4). The Nephilim were described as heroes and "warriors of renown" (Genesis 6:4). The Nephilim were people of unusually large stature with great physical abilities. They are mentioned in Numbers 13:32—33 and Deuteronomy 1:28; 2:10—11. Also see 1 Samuel 17:4—7 and 2 Samuel 21:16, 18—22.

Who were theses sons of God? What purpose do these verses have? Do they relate to Adam's genealogical table or to the flood story which follows? What meaning do they have for our spiritual lives today?

Traditionally, "the sons of God" (Genesis 6:2) have been viewed as divine beings who belonged to God's heavenly court.[50] The term has this meaning in the book of Job (1:6; 2:1; 38:7) and in the extracanonical books of the Book of Enoch and the Book of Jubilees. This interpretation is in keeping with the way the phrase "sons of" is used in the rest of Hebrew Scripture, e.g., the sons of Israel. This interpretation reflects an ancient story in which angelic beings intermarried with humans. Such intermarriage was a common feature among the gods of classical Greek mythology.

When the phrase "the sons of God" is understood in this way, these verses are linked to the flood story. They explain the origin of the Nephilim and, thereby, the increase in wickedness and evil that led to the destruction of the earth by the flood (Genesis 6:5). The increase of wickedness and evil came from outside of humanity. It had an external, heavenly source.

Another way of understanding the phrase "the sons of God" is as a reference to the descendants of Adam through Seth. This understanding links these verses to the genealogy which preceded them. It continues the contrast drawn between the lineage of Cain and the lineage of Seth. The descendants of Seth were those who were made in the likeness of Adam who was made in the likeness of God (Genesis 5:1—3). Thus, Adam's descendants through Seth would have been the sons of God. Seth's descendants were the ones who called upon the name of the LORD (Genesis 4:26) and who walked with God (Genesis 5:21—24).

In this understanding, the descendants of Adam who lived in relationship with God (i.e., the line of Seth) married the descendants of Cain who had no relationship with or inclination towards the LORD. In this intermarriage of the two lines, the shaping influence was the attitude embodied in the line of Cain. The inclination to walk in self-centered, self-reliance was greater than the inclination to walk in faithful obedience with the LORD.[51] The result was an increase in wickedness and evil rather than an increase in faithful obedience. The unusually long lifespans of Seth's descendants were impacted, as well. The LORD limited their lifespan to one hundred and twenty years.[52]

These two different understandings are reflected in the way Genesis 6:3 has been translated in different versions. The variation in translations is based on a difficult Hebrew word that has an uncertain meaning.

The NRVS translation focuses on the issue of human mortality—how long will humans live: "My spirit shall not *abide* in mortals forever, for they are flesh; their days shall be one hundred twenty years" (emphasis added). If we understand the intermarriage to be between heavenly beings and the daughters of humans, we might ask the question "will the offspring be eternal like the divine beings or mortal like their mothers?" This translation answers the question. The intermarriage with heavenly beings did not translate into even longer life. The LORD put a limit on how long we humans can live.

The NIV translation focuses on the relationship between the LORD and humankind. "My Spirit will not *contend* with humans forever, for they are mortal; their days will be a hundred and twenty years" (emphasis added). The relationship is viewed as a contentious one in which the LORD struggled with the self-centered, self-reliant spirit of humans. The man and the woman in the garden were the first to act out of such a spirit, bringing devastating consequences. Cain followed in their steps, bringing even more devastating decisions with dire consequences. The ultimate fruit of such a spirit was expressed in the vengeful attitude of Cain's descendant Lamech who sought unlimited, disproportionate retaliation for any wrong he experienced. Ultimately, living out of such a spirit produced the increase in wickedness and evil on the earth, expressed in violence. In this understanding, the reference to the one hundred and twenty years is seen as a period of the LORD's forbearance before the flood. It was the refusal to give up on humankind, giving them one more chance.

What meaning would these verses have had for the people of Israel living during the post-exilic period when the Hebrew Scriptures were collected and compiled? What meaning do these verses have for our spiritual lives today?

The post-exilic Jews would have likely read these verses as they read the other pieces recorded in Genesis 1—11. They would have been read against the backdrop of their failure to live in faithful obedience to the LORD, resulting in the loss of their homeland and their life in exile. They would have understood "the sons of God" as a reference to Seth's descendants. Thus, the verses could have been understood as a warning about intermarriage with non-Jews, supporting the kind of ethnic cleansing recorded in Ezra 9 and 10. These verses were for them, as well as for us, a call to live in faithful obedience to the LORD, following the ways of the LORD.

The Editor's Note

For the third time in Genesis, the editor used the phrase "these are the generations of" to indicate a progression in the story being told (Genesis 6:9). The story of creation gave way to the story of the garden which now gives way to the story of Noah.

Noah was described as "a righteous man, blameless in his generation" (Genesis 6:9). The word "righteous" means he lived rightly in his relationships with others. He was also blameless. No one had any basis for finding fault with him or with how he treated them. In addition, Noah, like his ancestor Enoch, walked with God. He enjoyed close fellowship with God as did the man and woman in the garden before their decision to disobey the LORD God's directive about the tree of knowledge.

This introduction of Noah is the opening of the E version of the flood story.

A Guide for Personal Reflection and Journaling, for Group Conversation and Discussion

1. What new thought or understanding did you gain through this introduction?
2. How does that new thought or understanding impact the way you read the story of the flood?

CHAPTER 18

RETURN TO CHAOS: THE STORY
OF NOAH AND THE FLOOD

I t takes four chapters to tell this familiar story of Noah and the flood. The story progresses along a natural storyline:

> God's decision to destroy humankind while saving Noah, Genesis 6:5—8 and 6:11—13;
> the ark, Genesis 6:14—22 and Genesis 7:1—10;
> the flood, Genesis 6:7:11—24;
> the end of the flood, Genesis 8:1—12;
> leaving the ark, Genesis 8:13—19;
> the covenant God made, Genesis 8:20—22 and Genesis 9:1—17;
> life after the flood: the curse of Canaan, Genesis 9:18—27;
> the death of Noah, Genesis 9:28—29.

God's Decision to Destroy Humankind While Saving Noah, Genesis 6:5—8 and 6:11—13

The story attributes the flood to God. Seeing the condition the world was in, God made the decision to destroy it.

The decision to destroy the world is first told from the J source (Genesis 6:5—8). The wickedness and evil of humankind were identified as the reason for the LORD's decision.

> The LORD saw that the *wickedness* of humankind was
> great in the earth, and that every inclination of the
> thoughts of their hearts was only *evil* continually. And
> the LORD was sorry that he had made humankind on
> the earth, and it grieved him to his heart (Genesis 6:5—
> 6, emphasis added).

This wickedness and evil reflect the spirit of unlimited, disproportionate retaliation voiced by Cain's descendant Lamech. (The story of Cain came from this same J source.) Wickedness and evil are the inescapable outcome of a spirit of revenge.

"The LORD saw" parallels the creation story in Genesis 1 where God saw that it was good. This parallel is repeated in the priestly source, as well (Genesis 6:12). What the LORD saw was wickedness, not that which was good as in the story of creation. The LORD saw wickedness that had become excessive. The degree of human wickedness is emphasized by piling up words to describe it: great, every, only, continually. The use of Hebrew parallelism defines wickedness as "every inclination of the thoughts of their hearts was only evil continually." Their imagination—the creative capacity that reflects the image of God—was being used for evil, not good. Their energies were given to planning destructive schemes rather than to bringing forth life and nurturing it. They were creating chaos rather than structuring order that allowed fullness of life to blossom. The phrase echoes the scheming of Cain in planning the murder of his brother Abel.

What the LORD saw in the heart of humankind impacted the heart of God. "And the LORD was sorry that he had made humankind on the earth, and it grieved him to his heart" (Genesis 6:6). The LORD's response to the depth of human wickedness was to grieve it. The Hebrew word translated "grieved" literally means "to heave a sigh." The LORD was not unaffected or unmoved by what He saw. It touched the LORD deeply, stirring grief and regret. It impacted the LORD, moving God to act. This biblical statement points to the LORD's deep connection with humankind

What the LORD saw led to a decision: "I will blot out from the earth the human beings I have created—people together with animals and creeping things and birds of the air" (Genesis 6:7). But in the midst of the wickedness and evil, the LORD also saw Noah. "But Noah found favor in the sight of the Lord" (Genesis 6:8).

The E version (Genesis 6:11—13) identifies a different reason for God's decision to destroy the earth with a flood. That reason had to do with the earth itself, rather than with humans. Humans had corrupted the earth so that it was filled with violence.

> Now the earth was corrupt in God's sight,
> and the earth was filled with violence.
> And God saw that the earth was corrupt;
> for all flesh had corrupted its ways upon the earth
> (Genesis 6:11—12).

Again, the "God saw" reference from the story of creation is used. The corruption of the earth which God saw stands in contrast to the good, very good description of creation found in the story of creation. (The story of creation came from the same source as this portion of the story of the flood).[53] The Hebrew word translated as "corrupt" means "destroyed." The creation that God had made and proclaimed *good* had been destroyed. It was filled with violence instead of goodness.

Violence is the use of power against another to attack, dominate, control, and destroy the other for one's own personal advantage. It devalues the other, treating them as an enemy to be eliminated. It demonizes the other to justify eliminating or destroying them. It was how Cain used power against his brother Abel.

Violence stands in contrast to the way God uses power. The story of creation shows God uses power to create. God used power to bring life into being and nurture it to maturity. Humankind used the creative powers God gave them in ways that were foreign to God's ways. Rather than using their creative powers to bring forth that which was good (as in Genesis 1), they used their creative powers to destroy. This abuse of power destroyed the earth. The impact of humankind's actions upon the earth reflects the link between the earth and humankind. It echoes the story of the garden when the ground was cursed as one of the consequences of the couple's decision to disobey the directives of the LORD God.

This description again highlights the progressive nature of sin in human life. The couple's decision in the garden to follow their own way evolved in the story of Cain to Cain's disregard of the LORD's warning. His disregard of what the LORD said led to an act of violence as Cain killed his brother Abel. Cain's act, coupled with his decision to walk away from the LORD, sowed the seed for the spirit of revenge out of which Lamech lived. Lamech sought unlimited, disproportionate retaliation for the wrongs he experienced. The spirit of revenge with its attitude of unlimited retaliation created a world full of violence. It created a world in chaos, returning the earth to its original condition (Genesis 1:2).

The Ark, Genesis 6:14—22 and Genesis 7:1—10

The situation had been evaluated, the condition identified, and a decision made. The story now moves to putting the decision into action.

The destruction God planned was not a total destruction. God spared Noah and his family, along with a pair of every living thing. God instructed Noah to build a three-storied ark that would protect him, his family, and two of every animal, creeping thing, and birds from the flood's destructive power. Through this small remnant, God would repopulate the earth. They represented a new beginning, the very thing for which Lamech, Noah's father, had longed.

Sparing the lives of Noah, his family, and two of every living thing is presented as God's covenant with Noah and all living things. "But I will establish my covenant with you" (Genesis 6:18). This statement is the first use of the word "covenant" in the Bible. Covenant is the central theme of the rest of the Hebrew Scriptures. The concept of covenant drives the story of Abraham and his descendants. Here, God's covenant is to keep this select group alive.

"Noah did this; he did all that God commanded him" (Genesis 6:22). Noah did what the couple in the garden failed to do. He lived in faithful obedience to God's directives. His faithful obedience allowed him to escape death in the flood.

The J version (Genesis 7:1—10) does not repeat God's instructions for building the ark. Rather, in this version, the LORD commanded Noah to go into the ark with his family and with the animals. Noah was instructed to take seven pairs of animals that were considered clean and one pair of those that were unclean. Two different times this version made reference to Noah's faithful obedience. "And Noah did all that the LORD had commanded him" (Genesis 7:5) and "as God had commanded Noah" (Genesis 7:9). The new beginning the flood brought began with humans once again living in faithful obedience to God.

This version indicated that Noah was six hundred years old when the flood waters came over the earth (Genesis 7:6).

The flood, Genesis 7:11—24

The flood is described in graphic terms that underscore its extent as well as its effectiveness in achieving the destruction of all flesh God intended.

The flood came about by the joining of two forces that God had separated in the creation story. Waters covered the earth before God began speaking into its chaos (Genesis 1:2). God divided those waters on the second day of creation, creating a dome that separated the waters beneath the dome—the seas—from the waters above it—the skies (Genesis 1:6—8). Then on the third day, God separated the waters below so that dry land appeared (Genesis 1:9—10). Here, those creative acts were reversed. The earth's fountains or springs burst forth as the rain from the sky began to fall. These combined forces returned creation to its original state of chaos (Genesis 7:11—12).

The exact time the flood waters began to build is noted (Genesis 7:11). That notation allows the author to specify how long the flood lasted. See Genesis 8:13—14.

The story details the severity of the flood, returning the earth to its original state of chaos:

> And the waters increased ... The waters swelled and increased greatly on the earth ... The waters swelled so mightily on the earth that all the high mountains under the whole heaven were covered; the waters swelled above the mountains (Genesis 7:17, 18, 19, 20).

The extent of the flood accomplished what God had intended. Less there be any doubt, the destruction of all life is stated twice. The second description specifically states that God "blotted out every living thing."

And all flesh died that moved on the earth, birds, domestic animals, wild animals, all swarming creatures that swarm on the earth, and all human beings; everything on dry land in whose nostrils was the breath of life died. He blotted out every living thing that was on the face of the ground, human beings and animals and creeping things and birds of the air; they were blotted out from the earth (Genesis 7:21—23).

The LORD's protective hand is mentioned throughout the account of the flood. As the flood began to unfold, "the LORD shut him in" the ark (Genesis 7:16). Then, in the midst of the destructive power of the flood, the story repeatedly mentions God's work of rescuing Noah, his family, and two of every living thing. As the waters increased, they "bore up the ark, and it rose high above the earth" (Genesis 7:17). As the waters swelled, "the ark floated on the face of the waters" (Genesis 7:18). As the waters swelled so mightily that all flesh was destroyed, "Only Noah was left, and those that were with him in the ark" (Genesis 7:23). Saving Noah and his family along with a pair of every living thing was as much the work of God as was the destruction of all of life on the earth.

"The waters swelled on the earth for one hundred fifty days" (Genesis 7:24). Once again, the waters of chaos covered the earth.

The End of the flood, Genesis 8:1—12

Having accomplished it intended purpose, the flood ended, allowing the new beginning to take place. Destruction is never the final word. New life is.

Before the flood, God saw. Then God said. And then God acted. Now, God remembered (Genesis 8:1). Noah and those with him were not forgotten. Remembering, God acted again. This time, God's action was to bring the flood to an end. "And God made a wind blow over the earth, and the waters subsided" (Genesis 8:1). Just as a wind from God blew across the face of the waters of chaos in the story of creation (Genesis 1:2), here a wind from God blew across the face of the waters of the flood, causing the waters to begin to recede. The two great sources that combined to fuel the flood—the waters of the fountains of the earth and the rain from windows of heaven—were restrained so that the waters could begin to recede (Genesis 8:2—3). After one hundred fifty days, the flood began to drain away. Just as the flood waters bore the ark up on their surface, now the receding waters settled the ark in the mountains peaks that began to resurface. After three months, the mountain tops were once again visible.

Seeing the tops of the mountain, Noah began to explore the condition of the post-flood earth. Noah first sent out a raven, but it did not return to the ark. So Noah sent out a dove. The dove returned to the ark because the waters still covered the earth. A week later, he sent the dove out again. This time, the dove returned with a freshly plucked olive leaf in its beak. The waters no longer covered the earth, allowing the trees and plants to begin to grow again. Noah waited another week, then sent the dove out yet again. This time, the dove did not return, indicating it had found a place to nest outside of the ark. The flood was over.

Leaving the Ark, Genesis 8:13—19

For eleven months, the waters of chaos covered the earth.[54] After the waters had receded, Noah stayed on the ark for nearly two more months to allow the earth to dry out (Genesis 8:14). Then God instructed Noah to leave the ark.

God had instructed Noah and company to enter the ark (Genesis 6:12—22). Now, God instructed Noah and those with him to leave the ark. The time of repopulating and replenishing the earth had come.

The Covenant God Made, Genesis 8:20—22 and Genesis 9:1—17

The climax of the story is the covenant God made after the flood. The point of the story is found in this covenant. Once again, two versions of the covenant are presented, the first from the J source and the second from the E source. The two versions differ in significant ways while declaring the same theme.

In the J account, Noah's first act after leaving the ark was to offer a sacrifice of burnt offerings to the LORD. This act reflects the Temple focus of the J source. The LORD found the sacrifice to be pleasing and responded by making a promise. (The word covenant does not appear in the J version.) The promise was a resolution the LORD made within the divine Self—"the LORD said in his heart" (Genesis 8:21)—about what he would and would not do in the future. It was a covenant—if we dare to use that word—the LORD made with himself. The promise was in reaction to the destruction of life by the flood.

"I will never again curse the ground because of humankind ... nor will I ever again destroy every living creature as I have done" (Genesis 8:21). The LORD's resolve reflects two regrets. The first regret was the curse the LORD God placed on the ground as one consequence of the couple's choice (Genesis 3:17). It reflects back beyond the destruction of great flood to the story of the garden. Lamech, Noah's father, expressed the longing for a relief from that curse at Noah's birth. His hope was that Noah would bring that relief (Genesis 5:28—29). The LORD's second regret was for destroying life on the earth through the flood. The story of the flood began with the LORD regretting having created humankind (Genesis 6:6). It ends with the LORD regretting having destroyed them along with every living creature on the earth. Destroying life is contrary to God's nature.

The LORD's regret is explained by the statement "for every inclination of the human heart is evil from youth" (Genesis 8:21). The evil inclination of the human heart was the reason the LORD decided to destroy the earth with a flood (Genesis 6:5—6). After the flood, that same inclination is the reason the LORD resolved never to do so again.

Underlying the problem of human wickedness (Genesis 6:5) was the condition of the human heart. By destroying humankind, the flood brought an end to their wicked behavior, but it did not end their (our) inclination toward evil. What was in the human heart was unchanged by it. Judgment in the form of the flood did not resolve the problem of the heart's inclination towards evil.

The statement of the LORD's regret can be understood as saying, "Well, that didn't work. I won't ever do that again."

The J source used poetry to explain the impact of the LORD's commitment within the divine Self:

> As long as the earth endures,
> seedtime and harvest, cold and heat,
> summer and winter, day and night,
> shall not cease (Genesis 8:22).

The E version of the covenant (Genesis 9:1—17) is a much longer version. It consists of a blessing (Genesis 9:1—7) and a covenant (Genesis 9:8—17).

The blessing draws from three of the previous stories. The story of creation is echoed as is the stories of the garden and of Cain. The blessing "Be fruitful and multiply, and fill the earth" is verbatim the blessing God gave to humankind in the story of creation (Genesis 1:28—31). The relationship the man and woman enjoyed with the animals in the garden (Genesis 2:18—20) was destroyed as fear replaced trust (Genesis 9:2). The animals were now a food source for humans along with the green plants (Genesis 9:3). A stipulation about blood and a reckoning for a life taken (Genesis 9:4—6) draws on the story of Cain. It was designed to restrict the violence that filled the earth (Genesis 6:11) by establishing an accountability for the murder of another. The stipulation called for a reverence for life. Each person has value because humans were created in God's image and likeness (Genesis 9:6; 1:26). The blessing to be fruitful and multiply is restated as the earth had to be repopulated after the flood had destroyed all of life.

God's covenant in the E source is with Noah and his descendants as well as with every living creature (Genesis 9:8—10). The heart of the covenant is God's promise to never again destroy the earth with a flood (Genesis 9:11, 15). This E version echoes the LORD's regret at having destroyed creation that was voiced in the J version (Genesis 8:21).

The covenant included a sign that served as a reminder of the promise. The reminder was for God as God continued to deal with humankind and the evil inclination of their hearts. "When I bring clouds over the earth and the bow is seen in the clouds, *I will remember* my covenant" (Genesis 9:14—15, emphasis added).

"I have set my bow in the clouds" has historically been understood as a reference to the rainbow. The rainbow never appears apart from clouds, i.e., water in the sky (one of the sources of the flood). It is created by sunlight shining through the water in the atmosphere. This understanding of "my bow" as the rainbow is supported by the reference to a rainbow surrounding the throne of God in the throne vision of Revelation 4. "And around the throne is a rainbow that looks like an emerald" (Revelation 4:3).

The original Hebrew word translated as *bow* is difficult for scholars to translate. This difficulty has opened the door to another way of understanding "my bow." The bow can be understood as a reference to an implement of war—the bow used to shoot arrows. This understanding views the flood as God's effort to destroy human wickedness by attacking it. It was God's attempt to destroy human violence by being violent. As we saw above, judgment did not solve the problem of what is in the human heart. Thus, God hung up his bow. God would no longer use judgment as the way to deal with human wickedness and violence.

This understanding of a God who refuses to use power violently and destructively aligns with the vision proclaimed by the prophets Isaiah and Micah in which implements of war—swords and spears— are beaten into agricultural tools—plowshares and pruning hooks. In their vision, the nations of the world abandon the ways of war, coming to Jerusalem to learn the ways of God. Just as God hung up his bow, so the nations would hang up their bows.

> In days to come the mountain of the Lord's house
> shall be established as the highest of the mountains,
> and shall be raised above the hills;
> all the nations shall stream to it.
> Many peoples shall come and say,
> "Come, let us go up to the mountain of the LORD,
> to the house of the God of Jacob;
> that he may teach us his ways
> and that we may walk in his paths."
> For out of Zion shall go forth instruction,
> and the word of the LORD from Jerusalem.
> He shall judge between the nations,
> and shall arbitrate for many peoples;
> they shall beat their swords into plowshares,
> and their spears into pruning hooks;
> nation shall not lift up sword against nation,
> neither shall they learn war any more (Isaiah 2:2—4).

Though this second way of understanding "my bow" is relatively unknown, it is in keeping with the people of Israel's understanding of God and of how God uses power.[55]

God's use of power to destroy—the story of Noah and the flood—stands in contrast to how God used power in the story of creation to create life and bring it to maturity. The Hebrew ancestors seemingly used this widely known story of a flood to reinforce their understanding of how God uses power. God does not use power to destroy life. God uses power to create life and bring it to maturity.

"Hmmm. That didn't work. I don't think I'll ever do that again."

Life after the flood: the Curse of Canaan, Genesis 9:18—27

The story of Noah and the flood did not end with the covenant God made following the flood. As the story of Cain reflected life after the garden, so a strange story about Noah reflects life after the flood.

The original purpose of the story seemingly was to explain the inequality among the various nations in the early history of the people of Israel. Specifically, it explained the relationship between the people of Israel in the Land of Promise and the Canaanites whom they defeated in taking possession of the land. The story served an additional purpose in the narrative the editor(s) created in weaving these ancient stories together. It illustrated that life after the flood was not significantly different from life after the garden. Humankind remained unchanged in spite of the flood.

The sons of Noah were the means by which the devastated earth was repopulated (Genesis 9:18—19). This reference to his three sons included a reference to Ham's son, Canaan. This identification of a grandson is unusual and a hint that he will become the focus of the story. The genealogies of Noah's three sons are presented in Genesis 10.

Noah worked the soil as did Adam and Cain before him. He is identified as the first to cultivate grapes, using them to make wine. As with previous stories, these facts are given to set up the story to be told. The story that follows echoes themes from the story of the garden, specifically, taking of fruit, seeing, nakedness, and the curse. The experience of the flood did not change the central themes in the story of humankind.

As might be expected, Noah enjoyed the fruit of his labor and, in doing so, became drunk. In his drunken stupor, he lay naked in his tent. His youngest son, Ham, the father of Canaan, "saw the nakedness of his father, and told his two brothers outside" (Genesis 9:22). The two brothers acted discreetly to cover their father's nakedness. The story is clear that they did not see their father's nakedness (Genesis 9:23).

When Noah roused from his stupor, he somehow realized what Ham had done. In anger, he placed a curse on Canaan, Ham's son (Genesis 9:24—25).

Our cultural background and Western orientation leads us to focus upon and pass a moral judgment on Noah because of his drunkenness. The story, however, reflects Hebrew culture by focusing on Ham and passing judgment on him (Canaan).

Ham did two things that drew condemnation. First, he saw his father's nakedness. The Levitical law included specific regulations about the nakedness of family members, particularly the nakedness of one's father. (See Leviticus 18:6ff.) Thus, in the ancient Hebrew culture, shame fell on the one who saw the nakedness of another whereas in our Western culture, shame is felt by the one who is seen naked.[56] In contrast to Ham's actions, the other two brothers covered their father's nakedness, doing so in a way that they would not see it, 9:23. Ham was also in the wrong when he told his brothers about seeing his father's nakedness. His report possibility included laughing about it and/or ridiculing Noah.

Noah's curse fell on his grandson Canaan even though the misstep belonged to Canaan's father Ham. The curse established a hierarchy among the brothers, placing Canaan in a subservient position. "Cursed be Canaan; lowest of slaves shall he be to his brothers" (Genesis 9:25). The curse justified the displacement of the nations in the land of Canaan during the conquest of the land.

Noah's curse of Canaan was paired with a blessing of Noah's firstborn son, Shem. The blessing was from "the LORD my God," linking Shem and his descendants with the LORD just as the lineage of Seth, Adam's son, was linked with the LORD. Abraham and his descendants came from Shem's line. The blessing of Shem would have been viewed as a precursor to the blessing of Abram (Abraham), the patriarch of the people of Israel (Genesis 12:1—3). Although the people of Israel traced their identity back to Abram (Abraham), these stories allowed them to trace their heritage back, through Shem to Noah, through Noah to Seth, through Seth to Adam and the garden. They were the people who walked with the LORD.

Noah's youngest son Japheth was included in Shem's blessing. Japheth was associated with God (Elohim), not the LORD. He was given space to live in relationship with and under the authority of his older brother Shem. Canaan was also his slave.

This story established the hierarchy among the sons of Noah: Shem was established in the dominant, first place position, Japheth the youngest fell next in the hierarchy, with Ham-Canaan as slaves. They were not a part of the hierarchy as they did not enjoy any standing in it. The hierarchy established in this story is reflected in the genealogical table of Noah in Genesis 10.

The editor(s) used the story of Noah's drunken stupor to show that life after the flood was not significantly different from life after the garden. How could it be? The spirit of humankind and the condition of the human heart were not any different from before.

The Death of Noah, Genesis 9:28—29

The story of Noah and the flood ends with the record of Noah's death when he was nine hundred fifty years old. The record of his death conformed to the pattern of the genealogical tables.

A Guide for Personal Reflection and Journaling, for Group Conversation and Discussion

1. What new thought or understanding did you gain about the story of Noah and the flood?
2. Did your understanding of the story change any? If so, how?
3. With what part of the story did you identity?

CHAPTER 19

MINING THE RICHES OF THE STORY OF NOAH AND THE FLOOD

Our familiarity with the story of the flood can blind us to the truths the story holds. As we read the story, we naturally look for and see what we already believe.

Another factor that impacts our understanding of the story is our understanding of God. How we view God will determine how we interpret the story.

Wickedness, Evil, and Violence

One of the truths often overlooked in the story has to do with violence. The story presents violence as evil.

The two different versions of the story of Noah and the flood give two different reasons for God's decision to destroy the earth (as previously noted). Both versions used Hebrew parallelism to identify the rationale for God's decision. The J version linked "the wickedness of humankind" with "every inclination of the thoughts of their hearts was only evil continually" (Genesis 6:5). The evil inclinations of the human heart produced wickedness. The E version linked "the earth was corrupt" with "the earth was filled with violence" (Genesis 4:11). Violence was what corrupted the earth. The two versions describe the same reality, using different terms. The evil inclinations of the human heart produced wickedness expressed in violence which destroyed the earth. Wickedness and violence were and are the same. Wickedness is expressed in violence. Wickedness and violence are expressions of evil which destroy life as God designed it to be.

We readily agree that human wickedness is evil, but are more reluctant to equate violence with evil. Yet, the story of the flood identified human evil as expressed in wickedness and violence as the factors that destroyed the earth. Both are evil. Violence, like human wickedness, is evil. We have difficulty hearing this truth.

Violence—using power over, down against another in order to defeat, control, or destroy them for our own personal benefit—has been a recurring pattern in human history. It is rooted in our basic human nature. It grows out of our anxiety-based thinking. The history of every nation is filled with stories written in the blood of the violence-filled struggle to survive. The history of our nation is the story of power used—often violently—to claim and settle new land. It was the way of the first settlers from Europe as they arrived on the Eastern seaboard. It was the way used in the ever-expanding push westward to the Pacific coast.[57]

Violence is woven into the fabric of our American culture—so much so that we hardly notice it. We are fed a steady stream of violence through news reports, TV shows, movies, novels, and video games. (Violence sells!) Violence was a central theme embedded in many of our earliest children's cartoons (think Tom and Jerry, The Road Runner, Popeye) even as it is the dominant theme of most modern video games. Not only are we accustomed to violence, it seems to me we *value* the use of force (violence) against those we view as a threat or as enemies.

We humans are seemingly addicted to violence. The story of Cain suggests it has been a part of our human experience since the beginning.

Violence is evil because it is the opposite of how God uses power. As we saw above, the story of creation teaches that God used power to bring life into being and to nurture that life into maturity. God uses power in life-giving, life-enriching, life-affirming ways. Jesus taught this same way of using power when he taught the way of the servant. He not only taught the way of the servant, he lived it (Mark 10:41—45; Philippians 2:5—11).

God created humankind in the divine image (Genesis 1:26), giving us the capacity to think, to choose, and to use power. We were created to use power the way God uses power—in life-giving, life-enriching ways. Living in faithful obedience is more than simply obeying God's directives (Genesis 2:16—17). It is living out of the image of God in which we were created. It is using power the way God uses power—in life-giving, life-enriching ways. Violence is the abuse of the power God entrusted to us. Violence uses our God-given power in life-depleting, life-destroying ways. It uses power over, down against another in an effort to defeat, control, or destroy them for our own personal benefit.

We use power violently out of our fear of being hurt just as Lamech used his power in unlimited, disproportionate retaliation as his means of protection (Genesis 4:23—24). We use power violently in an attempt to keep evil at bay. The fear that drives our thinking blinds us to the dynamics at play in using power violently. Using our power against those we fear makes us like them. We are no different from them in how we use power. Both sides use power over, down against the other in an attempt to control, defeat, or destroy the other for personal benefit. We become like those we fear and hate.[58]

In addition, using power against those we fear and hate perpetuates the violent use of power. The seeds of resistance, defiance, and rebellion are carried in every act of domination (power used over, down against another). Domination breeds rebellion. Violence breeds violence. Using power in an attempt to control chaos creates more chaos. It never creates the "good, very good" God created. The best that can be achieved through the violent use of power is stability—and a tenuous, temporary stability, at that! The violent use of power never produces peace. While it creates an advantage for those exercising the power, it is at the expense of those against whom it is used. It never nurtures life for all. It creates a win-lose situation. And the benefit that is gained, the stability that is created is always temporary and unstable. Resistance and pushback inevitably arise. This reality is true on every level of human relationship, from the parent-child relationship to the international level.[59]

The story of the flood identifies the heart as the source of human wickedness and the violent use of power. "Every inclination of the thoughts of their hearts was only evil continually" (Genesis 6:5). Violence is rooted in the heart. Its roots penetrate deep into the human psyche. We are like Cain, brooding over our pain, plotting how to get back at those who have hurt us (Genesis 4:5) and, like Lamech (Genesis 4:23—24), planning how to protect ourselves from ever being hurt again. Our experience of pain and our fear of experiencing such pain again stir a self-serving, self-focused spirit within.[60] Our pain and fear lead us to use our power to protect ourselves, including using our power against another that we view as a threat (as Cain did with Abel). Taken to the extreme, we become like Lamech, using power against another in unlimited, disproportionate retaliation.

We see this kind of disproportionate retaliation being played out in multiple places in our twenty-first century world: the drug wars in the countries of South America and Central America that follow the flow of drugs into the US; the gang wars on the streets of US cities (often drug related); the Israeli-Palestinian struggle in the Middle East; the terrorist attacks by radicalized groups (both foreign and domestic) against US interests; the Catholic-Protestant conflict of Northern Ireland; the authoritarian regimes of South America and Africa. In every one of these scenarios—and countless others just like them throughout the world—the thoughts and energies of those involved are given to plotting how to win by destroying those they view as their enemies. "Every inclination of the thoughts of their hearts was only evil continually" (Genesis 6:5).

The Hebrew prophets envisioned a different reality. They envisioned a world set free from war and violence (Isaiah 2:1—5; Micah 4:1—4; Isaiah 11:3b—10; 65:17—25). All of the nations of the earth would turn to Israel to learn the ways of God. Justice and righteousness—the ways of God—would become the ways of the earth. Power would be used on behalf of the powerless in life-giving, life-enhancing ways (Isaiah 1:17). Righteousness—living in faithful relationship in community—would replace the spirit of disregard expressed in Cain's question "Am I my brother's keeper?" (Genesis 4:9). The differences that are inherent to human community would be negotiated with an eye toward equity (Isaiah 11:3—4) rather than settled by the rationale that "might makes right."

The prophets repeatedly challenged the Hebrew nation, calling them to live the ways of God. They called for a nation that followed the ways of justice and righteousness. The story of Cain captures that challenge in a nutshell.

How power is used is a recurring theme in the Hebrew Scriptures. The theme is portrayed as a contrast between the ways of the world and the ways of God. The ways of the world are the ways of domination—power used over, down against another in order to defeat, control, or destroy them for personal benefit. They are the ways of violence.

Egypt and Assyria and Babylon embody the way of domination. The witness of the Hebrew Scriptures is God opposes those who practice domination by acting on behalf of those who are dominated and exploited. The LORD rescued the Hebrew people from slavery in Egypt and gave them the Land of Promise. The LORD delivered the Hebrew people from exile in Babylon, returning them to the Land of Promise.[61]

This contrast in how power is used is continued in the New Testament writings although it is often unrecognized. In the New Testament writings, Rome replaces Egypt and Babylon as the embodiment of the world's way of using power over, down against others. Jesus was the embodiment of God's way of using power in life-giving, life-enhancing ways. Jesus identified God's way of using power as the way of the servant. He taught and lived out of a servant heart. In his confrontation with power, he refused to become like those who used their power over, down against him, going so far as to die a violent death at their hands. He taught and lived the way of non-violence (Luke 6:27—38).

The book of Revelation picks up the vision of the Hebrew prophets of a world shaped by the ways of God. The final vision in Revelation with its three scenes of a new heaven and earth, a new Jerusalem, and a new garden (see again Chapter 12) is but another expression of their vision. The book was written to encourage the followers of Jesus who were being persecuted (dominated) by the agents of Rome in Asia Minor. The author assured them Rome—their Babylon, the Great Whore (Revelation 17—18) and the tool of the dragon (Revelation 12—13)—would be defeated by the Lamb (the resurrected Christ). The Lamb, leading the armies of heaven, would overthrow Rome-Babylon and defeat the dragon, but not through the violent use of power. The Lamb would be victorious through the power of God's truth: "from his mouth comes a sharp sword with which to strike down the nations" (Revelation 19:15a). God and the Lamb of God would be victorious, leading to a new creation patterned after the ways of God (Revelation 21—22). Assured of victory, the followers of Jesus could be faithful in their defiance of the ways of domination by following the grace-based, non-violent, servant ways of God that Jesus taught.

Because violence is rooted in the heart, a transformation of heart is necessary for us to embrace this non-violent, servant-oriented way of thinking that Jesus taught and lived. This transformation of the heart is the work of God through the indwelling power of the Spirit.

The Spirit works to recreate us in the image of God, engraining the character of God within us, creating a servant spirit in the core of our being. Jeremiah spoke of this transformation of the heart in his vision of the new covenant: "I will put my law within them, and write it on their hearts" (Jeremiah 31:33). Jesus identified the transformation of the heart as the core focus of the spiritual journey:

> It is what comes out of a person that defiles. For it is from within, from the human heart, that evil intentions come: fornication, theft, murder, adultery, avarice, wickedness, deceit, licentiousness, envy, slander, pride, folly. All these evil things come from within, and they defile a person (Mark 7:20—23).

The Spirit's work of transforming the heart was a central theme in the Apostle Paul's writings. "All of us are being transformed into the same image (of Christ) from one degree of glory to another; for this comes from the Lord, the Spirit" (2 Corinthians 3:18). He spoke of this transformation as "the renewing of the mind" (Romans 12:2) so that we have "the mind of Christ" (1 Corinthians 2:16; Philippians 2:5—11).

As the Spirit transforms the heart, how we view others and how we treat others changes. We begin to relate to others with patience and kindness, out of compassion and understanding rather than out of fear (Colossians 3:12—17). We welcome and embrace each and every person, regardless of how different they are, because we view them as a beloved child of God, created in the image of God (Galatians 3:26—28). We are quick to forgive the wrongs we experience from others. Following the teachings of Jesus, we practice unlimited forgiveness (seventy times seven, Matthew 18:21—22). We live out of a spirit of joy and peace (Galatians 5:22—23), laced with thanksgiving (Colossians 3:15; 1 Thessalonians 5:17—18), rather than out of a fearful spirit of scarcity. A spirit of humility makes us gentle in how we deal with others. We give freely and generously to meet the needs of others. We live out of a servant spirit, using out power—in all its many forms—to seek the good of others. We love as Jesus loved. We love those whom Jesus loved.[62]

Lest we miss it, let me restate it. This way of relating to others is the result of the Spirit's work in our lives, transforming our hearts. The transformation of heart the Spirit produces in us results in a change in how we view and relate to others.

Before the flood, "every inclination of the thoughts of their hearts was only evil continually" (Genesis 6:5). That inclination was not affected by the flood. It was still the condition of the human heart after the flood (Genesis 8:21). The flood did not solve the problem of the heart. The solution to the problem of the human heart comes through covenant, not judgment. Living out of steadfast, faithful love, the LORD uses divine power to transform the human heart, infusing it with the servant spirit of Jesus, thereby, freeing it from its obsession with violence and evil. That covenant relationship is the story told in the Hebrew and Christians Scriptures.

That Didn't Work: Second Thoughts about Judgment

God's judgment is the most common way the story of Noah and the flood is understood. The story itself sets up this understanding as both versions begin with God's decision to destroy the earth because of human wickedness (the J version) and the violence that had corrupted the earth (the E version). But the story's ending calls for a different understanding of the story.

Both versions of the flood story end by stating God's regret in destroying the world and with a divine promise to never again destroy creation. The E version states that promise in terms of a covenant:

> I am establishing my covenant with you and your descendants after you, and with every living creature that is with you, the birds, the domestic animals, and every animal of the earth with you, as many as came out of the ark. I establish my covenant with you, that never again shall all flesh be cut off by the waters of a flood, and never again shall there be a flood to destroy the earth (Genesis 9:9—11).

The rainbow was established as the sign of that covenant. This divine promise and covenant are the climax of the story. The central truth of the story is found in it.

The J version of the story clearly states that the inclination of the human heart was not changed by the flood. "I will never again curse the ground because of humankind, for the inclination of the human heart is evil from youth" (Genesis 8:21). While the flood destroyed every living creature, including humankind (except for those on the ark), it did not eliminate human wickedness and violence. Eliminating human wickedness and violence was the reason behind the flood. These patterns of wickedness and violence resurfaced along with the flowering of the repopulated earth because the inclination toward evil of the human heart was unchanged. Judgement did not change what was in the human heart.

The story of the flood teaches judgment does not change what is in the human heart. It is not effective in changing human behavior because it does not deal with the source of the behavior—what is in the heart.

We have difficulty hearing this message and embracing this truth—just as we have difficulty hearing and embracing the story's message that violence is evil. We are quick to speak of the flood as God's judgment against sin, but we generally overlook God's regret at having destroyed the world by the flood. Judgment, like violence, is too much a part of our experience to question it.

We first experienced judgment in our homes in the form of parental correction. Our experience of judgment in our homes was reinforced in the school systems in which we were educated. Judgment has been a part of every community in which we live. If we are honest, we would say judgment—embodied in the legal profession, law enforcement, the court system, and all the enterprises that feed off these professions—is big business. Even more, judgment is a part of the theology proclaimed in our churches. God's condemnation of the unrepentant sinner is a common theme in evangelical theology.

Given our experience, we have learned to accept judgment as normal and necessary. We have learned to rely upon judgment—the punishment of wrongdoing—to deal with wrongdoing. We believe judgment is necessary to change behavior and the one who does wrong. We use the fear of judgment—in our homes, in our schools, in our communities, in our churches—to motivate a change of behavior. We fear that, without judgment, our society and our world will dissolve into chaos. Like so many things we accept as normal and necessary, we fail to examine the effectiveness of judgment to do what we believe it can do.

Five interrelated components come together to produce judgment: a violation of some standard of right and wrong, a person (or group) who holds a position of authority, the use of power by those in authority to create some form of pain for those who have violated the standard, the objective of conformity to the standard or obedience to the one in authority, and merit-based thinking.

Judgment presumes a violation of some standard of right and wrong. The standard may be expressed or unexpressed, agreed upon or imposed. In the story of the flood, the identified violation was human wickedness and violence. Humankind followed the pattern of Cain and Lamech, using power to eliminate those they viewed as a threat and to retaliate against those they thought had wronged them. They used their power over, down against others for their own personal benefit. They abused the gift of power that God entrusted to them when God created them in the divine image. They used power in destructive, life-depleting ways rather than in life-giving, life-enriching ways.

Judgment presumes someone in a position of authority. They have the authority and responsibility to deal with the violation. In the story of the flood, that authority belonged to God. The LORD observed the wickedness and the evil inclinations of the heart that produced the wickedness (the J version). God saw how violence had corrupted the earth (the E version). What the LORD saw grieved God's heart, stirring regret at having created humankind (Genesis 6:6) and moving God to act to address the wickedness and violence.

Judgment occurs when the person in authority uses their power to punish the violator for their violation of the standard of right and wrong. This punishment involves some form of pain. In the story of the flood, punishment came in the form of the flood which destroyed humankind along with all living things.

The objective of the pain is to bring about conformity to the standard and/or obedience to the one in authority. It is an attempt to create stability in the community by controlling those who disrupt community and by eliminating their disruptive behaviors. The story of the flood declared that judgment, i.e., destroying the world by the flood, did not accomplish this objective.

These first four interrelated components are rooted in the fifth component: merit-based thinking. Merit-based thinking is earning-deserving thinking. Using the language of deserving, it rewards right behavior and punishes wrong behavior. Merit-based thinking is the kind of thinking inherent to our human condition. It is the kind of thinking by which society functions. It is the kind of thinking we have known through our many experiences of judgment. But it is not God's way of thinking or relating.

Judgment uses power over, down against another. As has already been stated, using power over, down against another is not the way God uses power. As the story of creation teaches, God uses power in life-giving, life-enriching ways. To use the language of Jesus, God uses power to serve. Using power over, down against another goes against God's nature.

In the divine promise-covenant to never again destroy creation, God rejected judgment as the way of dealing with human wickedness and violence. Instead, God chose a way that addressed the source of wickedness and violence. God chose a way that addressed the condition of the human heart. The story of the flood ends with God's covenant. God chose to live in relationship with us humans as the way to resolving the problem of human (our) wickedness and violence.

The LORD's commitment to live in relationship with humankind, in spite of our wickedness and violence, is not just the story of Noah and the flood. It is the story told in scripture. That larger story repeatedly tells us the LORD relates to us with steadfast, faithful love—the central component of the divine character. The LORD deals with our failure to live in faithful obedience by being slow to anger, by not giving up on us or abandoning us, and by forgiving us.[63]

Relating to us with steadfast, faithful love does not mean God disregards our wrongdoing. As we saw in the story of the garden, God gives us the consequences of our choices. The pain of those consequences teaches us to live in faithful obedience. The Apostle Paul referred to God's use of natural consequences as the wrath of God.[64] The wrath of God is not God's boiling anger unleashed on unrepentant sinners. It is a moral principle built into the fabric of life. It is a dimension of human free will. (See again **The Consequences of the Man and Woman's Choice, Genesis 3:14—19** in Chapter 9 and **For in the Day You Eat of It: Consequences, not Judgment** in Chapter 10.)[65]

The biblical witness teaches us one additional factor about judgment and God: the impact of judgment upon God. The natural consequence of unrepentant human wickedness and violence is destruction. The failure—or refusal—to learn from the pain of our wrong choices ultimately leads to self-destruction. The biblical witness is that God grieves this end and works to prevent it.

The story of the flood began with a reference to this grief: "it grieved him to his heart" (Genesis 6:6). The prophet Hosea, whose written prophecies centered on the love of the LORD for Israel, noted the prospect of judgment and destruction fanned the LORD's love into greater flame:

> How can I give you up, Ephraim?
> How can I hand you over, O Israel?
> How can I make you like Admah?
> How can I treat you like Zeboiim?
> My heart recoils within me;
> my compassion grows warm and tender.
> I will not execute my fierce anger;
> I will not again destroy Ephraim;
> for I am God and no mortal, the Holy One in your midst,
> and I will not come in wrath (Hosea 11:8—9).

Such grief over judgment is reflected in Jesus's experience of weeping over Jerusalem as recorded in Luke's gospel (Luke 19:41—44). Jesus wept for Jerusalem because of the destruction that was coming on them—a destruction they could have avoided had they only heeded the way that leads to peace. But they stubbornly followed their own wisdom rather than the ways of God. They relived the experience of the couple in the garden.

The ancient Hebrews used the story of the flood to teach us that judgment does not resolve the problem of human wickedness and violence. Judgment does not address the source of the problem—the condition of the human heart. They used the story to teach us that relationship (covenant), not judgment, is God's way of dealing with the problem of human wrongdoing.

The story of the flood calls us to reexamine our assumptions about judgment. It calls us to rethink the issue of judgment.

My Covenant

God chose to deal with the problem of human wickedness and violence by living in covenant relationship with us.

The word covenant was first used in the Hebrew Scriptures in the story of Noah and the flood (Genesis 6:18; 9:9—17). It would reverberate from that point through the history of the people of Israel, shaping their lives. Covenant with God was the foundation of Israel's self-understanding. It was the central theme of their scriptures.

Covenant speaks of living in committed relationship with another. The term proclaims how God relates to humankind (us), particularly to the people of Israel. In Hebrew scripture, covenant was always God's initiative and was grounded in God's steadfast, faithful love. The Hebrew word *chesed* is the word commonly used in the Hebrew Scriptures to speak of this love. The term captures two ideas: love and faithfulness. God's covenant love is steadfast. It does not waver or falter. It is also faithful. God never gives up on or abandons God's people. God's steadfast, faithful love (*chesed*) is a defining mark in the character of God revealed to Moses on Mt. Sinai (Exodus 34:6—7).

Covenant relationship, rooted in the LORD's steadfast, faithful love, was—and is—how the LORD deals with the problem of human (our) wickedness and violence. It is how God addresses what lies in the human heart.

The covenant love of God which has the power to transform the human heart is the larger story of which the story of the flood is a part.

Noah and the People of Israel

The people of Israel would have identified with Noah and his role in the flood story.

Out of all the people of the earth, Noah alone lived in faithful obedience to God. Like him, the people of Israel had been chosen out of all the people on earth to live in relationship with God. Noah, like Israel, was a small remnant among all the people of the earth. Noah was the means by which the earth was saved and repopulated. Israel saw themselves as a light to the Gentiles, the means by which the world would know the ways of God and, thus, be saved. "I will give you as a light to the nations that my salvation may reach to the end of the earth" (Isaiah 49:6).

The people of Israel would have seen the story of Noah as their story.

A Guide for Personal Reflection and Journaling, for Group Conversation and Discussion

1. What was your reaction to how the author equated violence with evil? Where is violence—the violent use of power—taught and "celebrated" within our society?
2. How are the violent use of power and the way God uses power different? What is the implication of that difference for the people of God? What does it call us to do?
3. What was your reaction to the author's understanding that the primary truth the story of Noah and the flood teaches is "judgment doesn't work?" What does your reaction tell you about your attitude toward judgment? If the story does not teach that truth, what truth does it teach?
4. How does covenant—God living in relationship with us— resolve the problem of "every inclination of the thoughts of their hearts was only evil continually" (Genesis 6:5)?

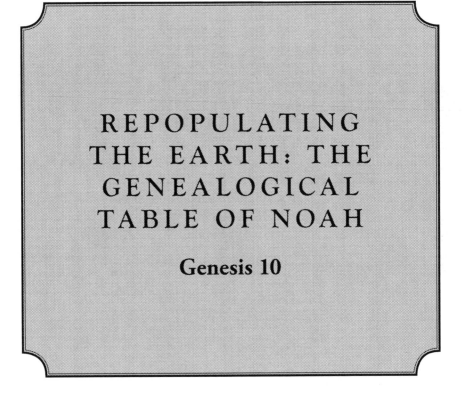

REPOPULATING THE EARTH: THE GENEALOGICAL TABLE OF NOAH

Genesis 10

Genesis 10

These are the descendants of Noah's sons, Shem, Ham, and Japheth; children were born to them after the flood. ²The descendants of Japheth: Gomer, Magog, Madai, Javan, Tubal, Meshech, and Tiras. ³The descendants of Gomer: Ashkenaz, Riphath, and Togarmah. ⁴The descendants of Javan: Elishah, Tarshish, Kittim, and Rodanim. ⁵From these the coastland peoples spread. These are the descendants of Japheth in their lands, with their own language, by their families, in their nations.

⁶The descendants of Ham: Cush, Egypt, Put, and Canaan. ⁷The descendants of Cush: Seba, Havilah, Sabtah, Raamah, and Sabteca. The descendants of Raamah: Sheba and Dedan. ⁸Cush became the father of Nimrod; he was the first on earth to become a mighty warrior. ⁹He was a mighty hunter before the LORD; therefore it is said, "Like Nimrod a mighty hunter before the LORD." ¹⁰The beginning of his kingdom was Babel, Erech, and Accad, all of them in the land of Shinar. ¹¹From that land he went into Assyria, and built Nineveh, Rehoboth-ir, Calah, and ¹²Resen between Nineveh and Calah; that is the great city. ¹³Egypt became the father of Ludim, Anamim, Lehabim, Naphtuhim, ¹⁴Pathrusim, Casluhim, and Caphtorim, from which the Philistines come.

¹⁵Canaan became the father of Sidon his firstborn, and Heth, ¹⁶and the Jebusites, the Amorites, the Girgashites, ¹⁷the Hivites, the Arkites, the Sinites, ¹⁸the Arvadites, the Zemarites, and the Hamathites. Afterward the families of the Canaanites spread abroad. ¹⁹And the territory of the Canaanites extended from Sidon, in the direction of Gerar, as far as Gaza, and in the direction of Sodom, Gomorrah, Admah, and Zeboiim, as far as Lasha. ²⁰These are the descendants of Ham, by their families, their languages, their lands, and their nations.

²¹To Shem also, the father of all the children of Eber, the elder brother of Japheth, children were born. ²²The descendants of Shem: Elam, Asshur, Arpachshad, Lud, and Aram. ²³The descendants of Aram: Uz, Hul, Gether, and Mash. ²⁴Arpachshad became the father of Shelah; and Shelah became the father of Eber. ²⁵To Eber were born two sons: the name of the one was Peleg, for in his days the earth was divided, and his brother's name was Joktan. ²⁶Joktan became the father of Almodad, Sheleph, Hazarmaveth, Jerah, ²⁷Hadoram, Uzal, Diklah, ²⁸Obal, Abimael, Sheba, ²⁹Ophir, Havilah, and Jobab; all these were the

descendants of Joktan. ³⁰The territory in which they lived extended from Mesha in the direction of Sephar, the hill country of the east. ³¹These are the descendants of Shem, by their families, their languages, their lands, and their nations.

³²These are the families of Noah's sons, according to their genealogies, in their nations; and from these the nations spread abroad on the earth after the flood.

CHAPTER 20

REPOPULATING THE EARTH: THE GENEALOGICAL TABLE OF NOAH

The three sons of Noah were how the earth was repopulated after the flood. The genealogical table found in Chapter 10 outlines that repopulation. It traces the descendants of Noah's three sons Shem, Ham, and Japheth along with the descendants of his grandson Canaan (Genesis 10:15—20).

The genealogical table recorded in Genesis 10 differs from the genealogical table of Adam recorded in Genesis 5. The Genesis 10 genealogy reflects people groups and nations rather than individuals. "These are the families of Noah's sons, according to their genealogies, in their nations" (Genesis10:32). The genealogical table of Adam recorded ages and the names of the firstborn sons and the number of years each ancestor lived. This genealogical table in Genesis 10 does not record ages. Its focus is on the people groups and nations that grew out of each of Noah's sons, not their individual lineages. The genealogical table of Shem, following the story of the tower of Babel, returns to the original formula used in Genesis for genealogical tables (Genesis 11:10—30).

The descendants of Japheth, Noah's youngest son, are identified first (Genesis 10:2—5). They are identified as the peoples of the coastal regions. They would have been the ancestors of the Philistines who were the enemies of Israel during the early years they lived in the land.

The descendants of Ham, Noah's second son, are listed next (Genesis 10:6—20). Ham was the son who saw his father's nakedness and whose son Canaan received Noah's father's curse (Genesis 9:22, 25). The descendants of his son Cush were the people associated with Egypt and northern Africa (Genesis 10:7) and with the Tigris-Euphrates River valley (the land of Shinar, Assyria, and Nineveh (Genesis 10:8—12). Both of these regions played important roles in the life of Israel. Egypt was the nation that enslaved the descendants of Jacob and was an ally against the nation of Assyria during the era of the divided kingdom. Assyria with its capital city of Nineveh was a warring nation that repeatedly invaded and eventually destroyed the northern kingdom of Israel. These nations that became the enemies of Israel were identified as the descendants of Ham who was cursed.

The descendants of Ham's son Canaan are also identified. The curse that Noah spoke against Ham was placed on Canaan. Canaan's descendants are the peoples whom Joshua drove from the land as the people of Israel entered the land of Canaan: the Hittites (Heth), the Jebusites, the Amorites, the Girgashites, and the Hivites (Genesis 10:15—20). Their defeat was interpreted as the fulfillment of Noah's curse on Ham/Canaan.

The descendants of Shem, Noah's first born whom he blessed, are listed last (Genesis 10:21—31). His lineage is presented in Genesis 11:10—30, linking the story of the Tower of Babel with the story of Abram. The people of Israel traced their heritage through Shem. This Genesis 10 genealogy identifies Shem as "the father of all the children of Eber" (Genesis 10:21), that is, the father of the Semitic peoples. The word "Eber" is an ancient form of the word Hebrew. Abram or Abraham, the father of the Hebrew people, came from these Semitic peoples. They came into the Syria-Palestine area between 1500 and 1200 B.C.E. They became the nations of Syria, Moab, Edom, and Israel.

This table in Genesis 10 sets the stage for the story of the Tower of Babel. "Cush became the father of Nimrod; he was the first on earth to become a mighty warrior. He was a mighty hunter before the LORD; therefore it is said, 'Like Nimrod a mighty hunter before the LORD.' The beginning of his kingdom was Babel" (Genesis 10:8—10).

THE STORY OF THE TOWER OF BABEL

Genesis 11:1—9

Genesis 11:1—9

Now the whole earth had one language and the same words. ²And as they migrated from the east, they came upon a plain in the land of Shinar and settled there. ³And they said to one another, "Come, let us make bricks, and burn them thoroughly." And they had brick for stone, and bitumen for mortar. ⁴Then they said, "Come, let us build ourselves a city, and a tower with its top in the heavens, and let us make a name for ourselves; otherwise we shall be scattered abroad upon the face of the whole earth."

⁵The LORD came down to see the city and the tower, which mortals had built. ⁶And the LORD said, "Look, they are one people, and they have all one language; and this is only the beginning of what they will do; nothing that they propose to do will now be impossible for them. ⁷Come, let us go down, and confuse their language there, so that they will not understand one another's speech."

⁸So the LORD scattered them abroad from there over the face of all the earth, and they left off building the city. ⁹Therefore it was called Babel, because there the LORD confused the language of all the earth; and from there the LORD scattered them abroad over the face of all the earth.

CHAPTER 21

THE STORY OF THE TOWER OF BABEL

The story of Babel is the fifth and last of the great epic stories in Genesis 1—11.

The story builds on and grows out of the repopulation of the earth through the sons of Noah. Because the repopulated earth descended from one family, they all spoke the same language. This fact is foundational to the story's plot. "Now the whole earth had one language and the same words" (Genesis 11:1). The story provides an explanation for the diversity of language and culture of the different people groups identified in the Genesis 10 genealogical table.

While Genesis 10 identifies the different people groups that descended from Noah's three sons, the identity of the people in this story is not specifically noted. The reference in Genesis 10:10 suggests they were descendants of Japheth through Ham and his son Cush who was the father of Nimrod. Nimrod's kingdom included Babel in the land of Shinar.

The setting of the story is identified as Mesopotamia. "And as they migrated from the east, they came upon a plain in the land of Shinar and settled there" (Genesis 11:2). "The east" is a reference back to the location of the garden (Genesis 2:8). "The land of Shinar" refers to the Tigris-Euphrates River Valley.

Come, let us …

The central theme of the story is the ambition of the people (Genesis 11:3—4). Their ambition was expressed in the twice repeated "Come!" The word calls them to work together to accomplish their plans. "Let us!" (Genesis 11:3, 4).

The first call was to bake clay in order to make bricks (Genesis 11:3). Bricks were the building material they would use in order to accomplish their second objective. Bricks and mortar reflect the desert region of the Mesopotamian setting. Rocks, such as would be found in the hills of Judea, were not as readily available in the Tigris-Euphrates River Valley. The manufacture of bricks reflects the kind of technical advancements attributed to Lamech's descendants (Genesis 4:20—22).

The second call was to build a city with a tower in it that would reach "into the heavens" (Genesis 11:4). For the ancient people, a city was a place to live together in community. A walled city provided safety. It was a place of refuge. This city was designed to provide an additional advantage: access to the realm of God.

The tower reaching into the heavens is the key feature of the story and the key to understanding it.

The ancient Hebrew people viewed the universe as a three-story house. The earth was the ground floor and the dwelling place of humankind. Under the earth—the basement—was the dwelling place of the dead. It was commonly referred to as the pit. The top floor was the heavens, the dwelling place of God. A tower with a top in the heavens would provide access to the realm of God.[66] Access through the tower would be like regaining access into the garden where God dwelled. Through the tower, the people sought to regain what the couple had lost in their expulsion from the garden. Through the tower, they sought to escape their situation just as Noah's father Lamech longed for relief from his situation. Through the tower, they sought, like the woman, to be like God, escaping the limits of their humanity. Through the tower, they sought to gain what belonged to God.

Their intention to build the tower was driven by a clearly stated purpose: "let us make a name for ourselves; otherwise we shall be scattered abroad upon the face of the whole earth" (Genesis 11:4). The people wanted to make a name for themselves. They wanted to be known for the great things they could accomplish. The people who died in the flood were known for how they used their power in wicked, evil, violent ways. These people after the flood wanted to be known for how they used their power to accomplish outstanding things.

On the surface, their desire—in contrast to that of the people who died in the flood—looked to be admirable. They were seeking to use their power to build something. In reality, the spirit that drove their project was no different from the spirit of those who died in the flood. Although the two groups used their power for different ends, they both operated out of the same self-focused, self-serving spirit. Those who died in the flood used their power over, down against others for their own advantage. They used the power in self-serving ways. These who built the tower also used their power in self-serving ways—"let us make a name for ourselves." Notice in their calls to work together the repeated use of "us, ourselves, we." Their focus was upon themselves—their designs, their desires, their ambitions. The common biblical term for this self-focused, self-serving spirit is pride. "Let us make a name for ourselves."

Their desire to be known for what they accomplished was a way of protecting themselves from being scattered over the face of the earth (Genesis 4:4). This fear of being scattered recalls Cain's life as a fugitive and a wanderer who had no place to be at home or safe or valued.

Their driving motivation was to avoid being scattered. In order to accomplish this intent, they sought to make a name for themselves by using their power to build. They sought to build a city with a tower that reached to the dwelling place of God. They began by making bricks to use in building the tower.

The LORD Came Down

In each of the five stories woven together in Genesis 1—11, The LORD was aware of what was happening. In the story of creation, God was aware of the watery, chaotic condition of the earth and spoke into it to bring forth structure and fullness. In the story of the garden, the LORD God was aware of the man and woman hiding in the garden, and sought them out. In the story of Cain, the LORD was aware of Cain's anger and sought to help him deal with it so that the anger would not dictate what he did. The LORD was aware that Cain had murdered his brother Abel and confronted him about his actions. In the story of Noah and the flood, the LORD was aware of the wickedness of human kind and the constant inclination of their hearts toward evil and chose to address it. In this story—the story of the tower of Babel—the LORD was aware of the building project the people had undertaken and the desires that fueled it. As in the other stories, the LORD acted out of that awareness.

A bit of humor coupled with irony is introduced into the story at this point. The people were building a tower to reach into the dwelling place of God yet God had to come down to see it. The language speaks of both the inadequacy of the project and its futility. The grand scheme of the humans was doomed from the start. They could not access the dwelling place of God.

The issue of one language is restated: "Look, they are one people, and they have all one language" (Genesis 11:6). The people's ability to communicate along with their God-given creative imaginations opened to door to limitless possibilities. "This (city and tower) is only the beginning of what they will do; nothing that they propose to do will now be impossible for them" (Genesis 11:6b). The stories of Cain and of the flood bore testimony to how humans used their creative potential in self-serving ways. These two stories chronicled how humans used power against one another in destructive, violent ways. In the story of the tower, they were attempting to invade the realm of God and usurp God's position. What other destructive, self-serving ways might humans use the great creative potential that God had placed within them when they were made in the divine likeness?

The LORD's solution was to take away that which opened the door to what they could accomplish: their common language. "Come, let us go down, and confuse their language there, so that they will not understand one another's speech" (Genesis 11:7). While the people were seeking to gain entrance into the dwelling place of God, the LORD visited them where they lived. The phrase "let us" reflects the royal court that surrounded the LORD and helped in the administration of creation.[67] The inability to communicate clearly undermines relationships. The inability to understand one another— even when we speak the same language—breeds suspicion and fear of the other. It creates chaos in the relationship, preventing us from working together. It often leads to conflict, resulting in alienation and division.

"So the LORD scattered them abroad from there over the face of all the earth, and they left off building the city" (Genesis 11:8). The very thing the people sought to avoid was they thing they experienced. They were scattered, isolated from one another. Their great project by which they sought to make a name for themselves was abandoned.

"Therefore it was called Babel, because there the LORD confused the language of all the earth" (Genesis 11:9). The word Babel means "gateway of God," reflecting the objective for the tower. The word "Babel" sounds like the Hebrew word for confusion. The English word "babble" refers to meaningless talking that is not understandable.

A Guide for Personal Reflection and Journaling, for Group Conversation and Discussion

1. What new thought or understanding did you gain about the story of the tower of Babel?
2. In what way do you identify with the story?

CHAPTER 22

MINING THE RICHES OF THE STORY
OF THE TOWER OF BABEL

These stories speak to us because they parallel our experiences in life. The story of the garden reflects our struggle with authority and inclination to be self-reliant rather than obedient to it. The story of Cain speaks to our struggle with those we view as rivals and with our anger about what we perceive they take from us. We can identify with the longing for things to be different, the longing for a new beginning expressed by Noah's father in the story of Noah and the flood. But what does the story of the Tower of Babel mirror back to us?

The desire that drove the people's ambition is a normal human desire. We all want to be capable and competent. We want to have the ability (power) to achieve something that is significant. This desire to achieve drives our creativity. It fuels our accomplishments, both individually and as communities. This desire is mirrored in our fear of being incapable, inadequate, or powerless. We loathe any appearance of failure or dependency on others.

As in the story, our accomplishments are a means to an end. They give us status and standing in the eyes of others as well as in our own eyes. They are the means by which we are respected and remembered. They are the means by which we "make a name for ourselves." In addition, they are how we connect to and contribute to community. They create for us a place to belong where who we are and what we can do is valued. Without these connections, we live isolated lives, disconnected and alone, even while living in the midst of community. We might just as well be scattered across the face of the earth.

The failure of the people in the story did not lie in this desire to achieve. The failure was in what they wanted to achieve: to invade the realm of God. They wanted what God had. They wanted to take the place of God. The biblical narrative refers to this desire as arrogance or pride.

Like the story of the garden, this story deals with the desire to escape the limitations of being human. In the story of the garden, the serpent appealed to this desire to entice the woman to eat of the fruit of the tree of the knowledge of good and evil. This desire to escape the limitations of being human lies at the core of what we call sin. The attempt to claim what rightfully belongs to God is the sin in this story. It grew out of a spirit of arrogance.

We all attempt to play God in our own ways. We like to be in control. We attempt to control others—what they do and what they think. We use what we believe as the standard by which we determine what is right. We reject anything that differs from what we think and condemn those who think differently. Believing our way is always best, we like things to be done our way and complain when they aren't. We try to bend life to our will and complain that life is not fair when it doesn't. All of these innate human traits are expressions of the same thing: the attempt to play God. They are indicators of the arrogance out of which we live.

We have difficulty identifying with the story of the Tower of Babel because we don't want to think of ourselves as arrogant. Arrogance is one of those things we recognize and condemn in others. We don't want to see it in ourselves.

The spiritual life involves two major challenges. The first is being at peace with and living within the limitations of our humanness. The second is using the power we do have in life-affirming, life-giving ways. Until we recognize and address these two challenges, we will inevitably use our power to build a tower that invades the realm of God. We will use our power to manipulate and control what we cannot control in order to bend the world to our will. As in this story of the tower of Babel and in the story of the garden, the result will not be what we thought it would be. Our efforts to play God—control what we cannot control—inevitably produce chaos and destruction in our lives as well as in the lives of those we love. Our attempt to control others destroys relationships rather than enriches them. It blocks our ability to communicate, creating confusion. As a result, we live isolated, disconnected lives, separated and scattered from one another.

A Guide for Personal Reflection and Journaling, for Group Conversation and Discussion

1. What have you accomplished or done that brings you a sense of satisfaction? What part did God play in that accomplishment?
2. In what ways do you recognize that you attempt to play God?
3. How have you made peace with the limitations of being human?
4. How do you use power in life-affirming, life-giving ways?

CHAPTER 23

PENTECOST: THE REVERSAL OF BABEL

In the previous stories, God did not abandon the individuals to the consequences of their choices—creation in chaos (Genesis 1), Adam and Eve (Genesis 3), Cain (Genesis 4). In spite of their failure to live in faithful obedience, God did not abandon them. God continued to provide and protect. God continued to act. The same is true in this tower of Babel story.

The story of the tower of Babel ends with the people unable to communicate, confused in their efforts, and consequently scattered abroad, alienated and separated from one another. But the LORD did not abandon the people to their state of confusion, alienation, and separation. God continued to act. As in the story of Noah and the flood, God acted by living in relationship—by making a covenant. The LORD called and established a covenant with Abram and his descendants (Genesis 12:1—3). Through Abram, the LORD intended to bless the world: "in you all the families of the earth shall be blessed" (Genesis 12:3b). The story of how the LORD walked in covenant relationship with Abram, working to bless the world through him, is the story of God not abandoning the peoples of the earth to their post-Babel condition of alienation and confusion.

The consequences that arose out of the tower of Babel experience were reversed in an event recorded in the New Testament book of Acts. The confusion of different languages was overcome. The alienation between peoples was overcome. A new project, in place of the tower reaching to the heavens, was undertaken. This reversal was the work of God. That event is known as the story of Pentecost (Acts 2).

The story of Pentecost records the outpouring of the Spirit on the followers of Jesus after his ascension. In his interpretation of the experience, Peter said it was the fulfillment of what the prophet Joel proclaimed: "I will pour out my spirit on all flesh" (Joel 2:28; Acts 2:17). The gift of the Spirit was a new, fuller expression of God's covenant to live in relationship with us humans. It was the means by which all the families of the earth would be blessed.

As the Spirit came on each of them, the disciples were able to speak different languages other than their native language (Acts 2:4, 7—11). The language barrier was overcome as was the confusion it caused. Beyond that experience, the Spirit taught the followers of Jesus to speak a universal language, God's language of self-giving, servant love. That language has the power to overcome the fear of how we are different that creates the barriers that divide us.

In addition, the alienation between the different ethnic groups was overcome (Acts 2:41—47). What began in that experience grew until the distinction between Jew and Gentile was overcome. As the Apostle Paul said, "in Christ Jesus you are all children of God through faith. There is no longer Jew or Greek, there is no longer slave or free, there is no longer male and female; for all of you are one in Christ Jesus" (Galatians 3:27, 29; also see Romans 4:16—25). The early church was a new kind of community in which social distinctions were set aside. Oneness and unity replaced alienation and division as the followers of Jesus took on what Paul called "the mind of Christ" (Philippians 2:5—11; 1 Corinthians 2:16). The journey into this oneness was not easy for the early church. It included struggle and conflict (see Acts 6:1—7; 10:34—48; 15:6—29). Paul's letter to the churches of Galatia was written to address the struggle in their congregations. But oneness and unity in Christ Jesus was a central principle in their life together (see Ephesians 2:11—22; 4:1—6 and 1 Corinthians 12:4—27).

In the tower of Babel story, humans conceived, designed, and implemented a project to invade the realm of the gods—"a tower with its top in the heavens"—as a means of making a name for themselves (Genesis 11:4). The LORD sabotaged that effort by confusing their language. As a result, the people abandoned their effort. In place of that effort, the LORD invited them—through the covenant with Abram (Abraham) and his descendants—to be a part of a bigger project. The LORD invited them to be a part of a project God designed, a project that would glorify God's name, a project that would bring oneness to all of the earth (Isaiah 2:2—5; 11:1—10; 49:6; 65:17—25) and to all of creation (Philippians 2:5—11; Ephesians 1:10; 3:8—11), a project in which they would share God's nature and participate in God's life. The LORD invited them to be partners in God's eternal redemptive purpose.

God's eternal redemptive purpose is a venture the LORD designed before the creation of the world: "just as he chose us in Christ *before the foundation of the world*," Ephesians 1:4, (emphasis added). God's objective in this divine enterprise is to unify everything in creation under the Lordship of Jesus, the Christ. God "made known to us the mystery of his will, ... as a plan for the fullness of time, to gather up all things in (Christ Jesus), things in heaven and things on earth," Ephesians 1:10. The term translated as "gather up" was a military term used during battle. It referred to a call in the heat of the battle for the warriors engaged throughout the battlefield to regather around the king or general. It was a call to regroup as one army. God's eternal redemptive purpose is to restore unity to creation—things in heaven (the dwelling place of God) and things on earth (the dwelling place of humans). The story of the garden (Genesis 3) points to the division and brokenness of creation as the couple was expelled from the garden. The oneness of heaven and earth—the spiritual realm and the physical realm—was broken. Humans no longer walked with God. God's eternal redemptive purpose is to heal the brokenness that runs through creation and is reflected in human relationships. It is to create a world filled the peace (shalom) and abundance reflected in the first part of the garden story (Genesis 2). God is at work creating a new heaven and a new earth in which God once again lives with God's people (Isaiah 65:17—25; Revelation 21:1—22:5; see again Chapter 12, "The Story of the Garden in the New Testament"). This new heaven and new earth are patterned after the nature of God and follow the ways of God (Revelation 21:23—24; 22:5). Jesus spoke of this God-shaped world as the kingdom of God.

Central to God's eternal redemptive purpose is Jesus's death and resurrection. His death and resurrection proclaim God's forgiveness that redeems us out of the death brought about by sin (Ephesians 1:7; 2:4—7). Because of his death on the cross, God has exalted Jesus as Lord (Philippians 2:5—11; Ephesians 2:21—22) and is working to "gather up" all things under his lordship (Ephesians 1:10, 22; 2:6; 4:1—6).

Our partnership is an essential element in God's eternal redemptive purpose. God has chosen to not work apart from us. Our role in God's project is to live in relationship with God as the followers of Jesus, learning and living the ways of God Jesus taught. In the language of the garden story, our role is to live in faithful obedience. As we live God's ways of grace and forgiveness, we are Exhibit B of God's ways. (Jesus was/is Exhibit A, Ephesians 2:7.) The rest of the world as well as the larger creation (see again Ephesians 3:10) will see in us the beauty and wisdom of God's ways and be drawn to them (Isaiah 2:2—5).

At Pentecost, the Spirit which brooded over the face of chaos in the creation story was poured out on the followers of Jesus, empowering them to live the ways of God Jesus taught in faithful obedience. They became the dwelling place of God on earth (Ephesians 2:21—22). That same Spirit empowers us, the followers of Jesus today. Living in us, the Spirit broods over the chaos of our post-Babel existence to bring forth God's new heaven and new earth that Jesus called the kingdom of God. We are God's partners in this eternal, redemptive enterprise of bringing God's kingdom on earth, as it is in heaven (Matthew 6:10).

In the story of the tower of Babel, people used their God-given creativity to build a tower that reached to the heavens. In their project, the LORD recognized the potential they had: "this is only the beginning of what they will do; nothing that they propose to do will now be impossible for them" (Genesis 11:6). What might we accomplish if we, using our God-given creativity and abilities, worked together under the guidance of the Spirit to build a group or a community or a society or a world patterned after the ways of God?

A Guide for Personal Reflection and Journaling, for Group Conversation and Discussion

1. What is your reaction to this interpretation of the reversal of Babel?
2. How would you describe God's eternal redemptive purpose? How does your understanding compare to the author's understanding presented in this chapter?
3. How would you describe your post-Babel existence?
4. What is your vision of what we might accomplish if we, using our God-given creativity and abilities, worked together under the guidance of the Spirit to build a group or a community or a society or a world patterned after the ways of God?

FROM THE TOWER OF BABEL TO ABRAM: THE GENEALOGICAL BRIDGE OF SHEM

Genesis 11:10—32

Genesis 11:10—32

These are the descendants of Shem.

When Shem was one hundred years old, he became the father of Arpachshad two years after the flood; [11]and Shem lived after the birth of Arpachshad five hundred years, and had other sons and daughters.

[12]When Arpachshad had lived thirty-five years, he became the father of Shelah; [13]and Arpachshad lived after the birth of Shelah four hundred three years, and had other sons and daughters.

[14]When Shelah had lived thirty years, he became the father of Eber; [15]and Shelah lived after the birth of Eber four hundred three years, and had other sons and daughters.

[16]When Eber had lived thirty-four years, he became the father of Peleg; [17]and Eber lived after the birth of Peleg four hundred thirty years, and had other sons and daughters.

[18]When Peleg had lived thirty years, he became the father of Reu; [19]and Peleg lived after the birth of Reu two hundred nine years, and had other sons and daughters.

[20]When Reu had lived thirty-two years, he became the father of Serug; [21]and Reu lived after the birth of Serug two hundred seven years, and had other sons and daughters.

[22]When Serug had lived thirty years, he became the father of Nahor; [23]and Serug lived after the birth of Nahor two hundred years, and had other sons and daughters.

[24]When Nahor had lived twenty-nine years, he became the father of Terah; [25]and Nahor lived after the birth of Terah one hundred nineteen years, and had other sons and daughters.

[26]When Terah had lived seventy years, he became the father of Abram, Nahor, and Haran.

[27]Now these are the descendants of Terah.

Terah was the father of Abram, Nahor, and Haran; and Haran was the father of Lot. [28]Haran died before his father Terah in the land of his birth, in Ur of the Chaldeans. [29]Abram and Nahor took wives; the name of Abram's wife was Sarai, and the name of Nahor's wife was Milcah. She was the daughter of Haran the father of Milcah and Iscah. [30]Now Sarai was barren; she had no child. [31]Terah took his son

Abram and his grandson Lot son of Haran, and his daughter-in-law Sarai, his son Abram's wife, and they went out together from Ur of the Chaldeans to go into the land of Canaan; but when they came to Haran, they settled there. [32]The days of Terah were two hundred five years; and Terah died in Haran.

CHAPTER 24

FROM THE TOWER OF BABEL TO ABRAM: A GENEALOGICAL BRIDGE

" These are the descendants of Shem" (Genesis 11:10). Once again we encounter the editor's note, indicating a shift in the story.[68] The genealogy is that of Shem, the one son of Noah associated with the LORD (Genesis 9:26). The pattern of the genealogy is like the genealogy of Adam found in Genesis 5. This genealogy reflects a decreasing life span in keeping with Genesis 6:3.

Shem's genealogy is the bridge from these ancient stories to Terah, the father of Abram with whom God established a covenant and through whom God worked to bring healing to creation. God's call of Abram is recorded in Genesis 12:1—3.

> Now the LORD said to Abram, "Go from your country and your kindred and your father's house to the land that I will show you. I will make of you a great nation, and I will bless you, and make your name great, so that you will be a blessing. I will bless those who bless you, and the one who curses you I will curse; and in you all the families of the earth shall be blessed" (Genesis 12:1—3).

Not surprisingly, this call to live in covenant relationship with the LORD reflects aspects of the story of Babel. "I will make of you a great nation" (Genesis 12:2) echoes "let us build ourselves a city," (Genesis 11:4). "I will make your name great" (Genesis 12:2) echoes "let us make a name for ourselves," (Genesis 11:4). "You will be a blessing" to others (Genesis 12:2) stands in contrast to the people's focus on themselves—us, ourselves, we (Genesis 11:4). "In you all the families of the earth shall be blessed" (Genesis 12:3) reverses "the LORD scattered them abroad over the face of the earth," (Genesis 11:8 and 9).

In addition, Abram's call echoes the five ancient stories of Genesis 1—11. The call portrays the LORD as a God who blesses as in the story of creation (Genesis 1:1-2:3). The call was for Abram to walk faithfully in relationship with God as the couple failed to do in the story of the garden (Genesis 3). The call included a promise to provide a land for Abram and his descendants just as the LORD God provided the garden for the couple in the story of the garden (Genesis 2). Abram and his descendants would not be fugitives wandering the earth as was Cain (Genesis 4:16). The call was for Abram to be a blessing to others rather than using power violently like Cain (Genesis 4:1—16) and his descendant Lamech (Genesis 4:23—24). The call was to a covenant relationship with the LORD as the way to address the problem of the human heart reflected in the story of Noah (Genesis 6:5—9:17). The LORD invited Abram to be a partner in God's project to bless all the peoples of the world. That invitation stands in contrast to the failed tower-to-heaven project in the story of the Tower of Babel (Genesis 11:1—9).

The story of Abram and his descendants is the story of Israel, a people seeking to live in covenant relationship with God, walking in faithful obedience. But their story is really the story of the LORD's steadfast, faithful love that refused to give up on them or abandon them even though they followed their own wisdom—like the couple in the garden—rather than walk in trusting, faithful obedience. In these five ancient texts, the people of Israel saw their story as the story of the LORD's steadfast, faithful love.

May we find our story in their story and in the story of the LORD's steadfast, faithful love!

A Guide for Personal Reflection and Journaling, for Group Conversation and Discussion

1. What new thought or understanding did you gain from this third genealogical bridge?
2. Where did you see yourself and your experience in these five ancient narratives?
3. What is your "take away" from this mining expedition of Genesis 1—11?

END NOTES

1. The Enlightenment was a revolution in thinking that took place in Europe during the late 17th and early 18th centuries. It was rooted in the development of science with its effort to understand the mysteries of creation. The foundational principle of the Enlightenment was human reason.

2. In our speculation, we come up with an answer to our own question. Our answer is based on our assumptions and understanding. Thus, our answers not only reflect our thinking, they reinforce what we already think. We create a self-reinforcing, closed-loop thinking process.

3. Pentateuch is a technical term meaning the five books.

4. All scripture quotations are from the New Revised Standard Version, unless otherwise noted. (copyright © 1989 the Division of Christian Education of the National Council of the Churches of Christ in the United States of America. Used by permission.)

5. Nothing in this poetic narrative is scientific in its orientation. It does not attempt to describe the process of how creation came into being—a scientific issue. Rather, it communicates that creation was the work of God. But it has an even greater message to communicate, as this chapter will reveal.

6. Hebrew parallelism is a common characteristic of Hebrew poetry. Parallelism refers to the relationship between two or more lines of poetry. It can also be a way of communicating and emphasizing an idea. Parallelism can take many forms. The most common form is when line A is restated, using different words, in line B. See Psalm 25:3—5. In another form, line B states a contrast to line A. For example, "cease to do evil" (Isaiah 1:16) stands over against "learn to do good" (Isaiah 1:17). Isaiah 1:17 is an example of parallelism used to emphasize a thought by adding one image onto another. Justice is to rescue the oppressed and to defend the orphan and to plead for the widow. In the Genesis 1 story of creation, the first three days of creation stand in parallel with the second three days.

7. Walter Bruggemann, Genesis in Interpretation: A Bible Commentary for Teaching and Preaching (Atlanta: John Knox Press, 1982), page 32.

8. Ibid., 37.

9.   The writer of Hebrews spoke of God's rest as a present reality. He urged his readers to pursue God's Sabbath rest, i.e., the spiritual maturity that God desires for us (Hebrews 4:9—11).

10. In addition to blessing the Sabbath, God also blessed the fishes and birds, commanding them to be fruitful and multiply (Genesis 1:22), and the man and the woman as they were entrusted with the care of creation.

11. To bless and to hallow is another example of Hebrew parallelism.

12. Compare Romans 8:19, Ephesians 1:3-14 and Colossians 1:16.

13. See again Chapter 1.

14. Faithful obedience was a dominant theological motif in ancient Israel. It is the central theme of the book of Deuteronomy and the history written from its perspective (Deuteronomistic history: the books of Joshua, Judges, 1 & 2 Samuel, 1 & 2 Kings). Deuteronomy used *if … then* language to teach its central theme: faithful obedience led to life and prosperity in the land while disobedience produced death and the loss of the land. This emphasis on faithful obedience and the blessing it brings is clearly expressed in Deuteronomy 30:15—20: "See, I have set before you today life and prosperity, death and adversity. *If* you obey the commandments of the LORD your God that I am commanding you today, by loving the LORD your God, walking in his ways, and observing his commandments, decrees, and ordinances, *then* you shall live and become numerous, and the LORD your God will bless you in the land that you are entering to possess. But *if* you heart turns away and you do not hear, but are led astray to bow down to other gods and serve them, I declare to you today that you shall perish; you shall not live long in the land that you are crossing the Jordan to enter and possess. I call heaven and earth to witness against you today that I have set before you life and death, blessings and curses. Choose life so that you and your descendants may live, loving the LORD your God, obeying him, and holding fast to him; for that means life to you and length of days, so that you may live in the land that the LORD swore to give to your ancestors, to Abraham, to Isaac, and to Jacob" (emphasis added). Tying life to faithful obedience and death to disobedience is also found in Deuteronomy 4:23—27, 39—40; 5:32—33; 6:3, 24; 8:19—20; 11:26—28. The theology of Deuteronomy was one way the nation's experience of exile was explained. Because they failed to faithfully follow God's law, their nation was destroyed by the armies of Babylon and the people were carried away to live as exiles in Babylon. The story of the garden is another expression of this theological perspective. It explains the reason for the exile in a nutshell.

15. Shame and guilt are both part of the family of emotions known as grief, but they are significantly different. Guilt is about behavior. It is the sense of grief over some wrong doing and the pain it has caused. Whereas guilt is about doing, shame is about being. It is the sense of being flawed and no good. It carries with it the fear of being unlovable. It plays on the fear of being rejected because we are unacceptable and unwanted. The wrong doing we committed (behavior) is evidence in our minds of our deeply flawed,

unlovable nature (being). Our failure to measure up to society's expectations proves to us that we are no good. The pain (grief) we feel about ourselves is called shame.

16. Some see in this statement a foreshadowing of Christ who would defeat Satan (Revelation 12). Such a reading is an example of reading our New Testament shaped belief back into the Hebrew Scriptures. It is foreign to the original story and a diversion to the story's original message.

17. This feature may have been the ancient's attempt to explain why childbearing was such a painful experience.

18. 1 Corinthians 14:33b—35 and 1 Timothy 2:11—15 are two texts attributed to Paul that reflect culturally governed, male hierarchy in the early church. Many biblical scholars today believe they are not originally from Paul.

19. The Apostle Paul echoed this understanding in his letter to the churches of Roman. See Romans 8:19—22.

20. Describing judgment as an expression of God's anger is an example of creating God in our image (see **Creating God in Our Image**, Chapter 4). We react with anger to another's disobedience, so we assume God does as well. It seems that grief, not anger, is God's reaction to our failure to live out of faithful obedience. God takes no pleasure in the painful consequences we experience for the choices we make. For the grief of God see "The Pathos of God" in The Prophets by Abraham Heschel (1962).

21. See Exodus 34:6—7 where the steadfast, faithful love of God (*chesed*) is identified as a dimension of the divine character. That love extends to the thousandth generation, that is, without end. Also see Hosea 11:8—9 where God's compassion is fanned into blazing hot flame at the thought of judgment.

22. In Exodus 34:6—7, the LORD is described as "a God merciful and gracious."

23. The restatement of the expulsion from the garden, using two different terms, is an expression of Hebrew parallelism.

24. *Either-or thinking* is inherent to our Western, scientific-oriented thinking. This way of thinking often creates false dichotomies and false issues. The controversy over creationism versus evolution is one example.

25. The Holy Bible, New International Version®, NIV® (Copyright © 1973, 1978, 1984, 2011 by Biblica, Inc.™ Used by permission. All rights reserved worldwide.)

26. Our emotional-spiritual growth comes through challenge. Our response to the challenge is a major factor in what God can do through it and in how we will grow through it.

27. Psalm 103 is based on the LORD's revelation of the divine character found in Exodus 34:6—7. Verses 7 & 8 of the psalm quote the Exodus text.

28. See the last part of Exodus 34:7, "yet by no means clearing the guilty, but visiting the iniquity of the parents upon the children and the children's children, to the third and the fourth generation."

29. This kind of dualistic thinking first surfaced in Hebrew writings during the post-exilic period. It reflects Persian influence.

30. See <u>The Pentateuch and Haftorahs</u>, J. H. Hertz, editor; 2nd edition (1937), page 196.

31. In contrast to Sirach, the Apostle Paul tied the entrance of sin and death to Adam, Romans 5:12—21. Paul's comments were theological, not historical. They were a part of an analogy he drew between Adam and the Second Adam, Christ Jesus.

32. Many modern scholars do not view Paul as the author of the books of 1 & 2 Timothy. The perspective expressed in this verse is at odds with other statements of Paul in books that are undoubtedly from him.

33. In the Transfiguration experience (Mark 9:2—8), this veil that separates the physical from the spiritual was pulled aside so that the three disciples could see the spiritual dimension that infuses the physical. They saw the more-than-the-physical life Jesus would enter through his death.

34. Mystic spirituality continually calls us beyond the arbitrary, artificial distinction between the sacred and the secular. It calls us to recognize the sacred in the secular, the spiritual in the physical. It calls us to embrace all of life as sacred and, thereby, all people as people of sacred worth. It calls us beyond us-them divisions.

35. The use of liturgical readings in mainline Christian churches is patterned after this practice. These liturgical readings include readings from the Law, the Prophets, and the Psalms as in the synagogue with the addition of readings from the Gospels and the Epistles.

36. See N. T. Wright, <u>Surprised by Scripture: Engaging Contemporary Issues</u>.

37. In scripture, this attitude of self-reliance is called pride, arrogance, or a lack of faith.

38. For the four different identifiable sources used in compiling the Pentateuch, see again the discussion at the end of Chapter 1.

39. See again the comments related to Genesis 3:20.

40. Compare Psalm 4:4 and Ephesians 4:26. What we do in our anger, not the emotion of anger, is where the sin lays.

41. The protection the mark provided for Cain corresponds to the six cities of refuge that were established for fugitives when the people of Israel first entered the Land of Promise. These cities provided protection for those who fled to them. See Numbers 35:6, 9—15; Deuteronomy 4:41—43; 19:1—10; Joshua 20:1—9.

42. Firstborns often do not recognize their privileged status because it is their "norm." Like Cain in the story, they have never known what it is like to not be valued or powerful.

43. See Isaiah 1:17 and 61:8.

44. See Isaiah 2:2—4; 11:1—9; 61:1—8.

45. Scapegoats are easily seen in the political realm as both political parties view the other as what is wrong with our country. African-Americans, Asians, Hispanics, immigrants, members of the LGBTQ community, and Moslems have historically been targeted as scapegoats in our culture.

46. People who feel powerless often blame those in positions of power and affluence as the problem.

47. I intentionally link these three terms together in order to convey how these three dimensions are interrelated. Progress in one of these areas will lead to progress in the other two.

48. See again Chapter 1.

49. See again the introduction where our scientifically-oriented thinking is addressed.

50. An early, ancient understanding of God was modeled after the people's understanding of their king. Just as a king had trusted members of his court, so God as the heavenly king had trusted members who helped govern the world. In post-exilic times and later, these members of the heavenly court were called angels.

51. This understanding calls to mind the Apostle Paul's warning about marriage between believers and unbelievers (2 Corinthians 6:14).

52. Moses was one hundred and twenty when he died (Deuteronomy 34:7).

53. Note that in both accounts of the decision to destroy the world, the reason given for the decision was in harmony with the previous stories from that same source.

54. Compare Genesis 7:11 with Genesis 8:13.

55. I first heard this interpretation from the Rev. Dr. Lisa Neslony, senior pastor of St. John the Apostle United Methodist Church of Arlington, Texas, in her sermon on the second Sunday of Lent, February 21, 2021.

56. This cultural practice helps to explain Jesus's instructions in Matthew 5:40 and Luke 6:29. When a creditor sued for a person's coat (outer garment), the one being sued had no other possessions that could be taken. He was in abject poverty, a position of shame. Jesus's instruction to give the creditor the cloak (the inner garment) as well would have made the one being sued naked before the court. As shame went to the one viewing the nakedness, this act would have shifted the shame from the one being sued to the creditor and judge who used their power to take advantage of the man. Jesus's instructions were an example of nonviolent resistance that challenged the abuse of power and position in society. See Walter Wink, Engaging the Powers: Discernment and Resistance in a World of Domination, Fortress Press, 1992, page 371.

57. This violent use of power is reflected in how we speak of "the wild west" and to the use of the six gun to tame it.

58. Becoming like the one we fear/hate is an overlooked fallacy in most good versus evil stories, e.g., Star Wars, Harry Potter, The Lord of the Rings.

59. Walter Wink spoke of the cycle of domination and resistance as the myth of redemptive violence. See again his book Engaging the Powers: Discernment and Resistance in a World of Domination.

60. We saw in the story of the garden how fear produced a self-serving spirit. The fear of missing out kindled a self-centered, self-serving, self-reliant spirit in the couple, leading them to disobey the LORD God's directive.

61. The Hebrew Scriptures revolve around these two "exodus" stories. These two events shaped Israel's self-understanding as well as their understanding of God.

62. Living out of a servant spirit does not mean we allow others to take advantage of us or abuse us. (Both are expressions of power used to dominate). The ability to love requires a healthy sense of self. It is dependent upon healthy boundaries. Without healthy boundaries, we assume responsibility for what rightfully belongs to another. We attempt to control what they do or don't do. We attempt to change them to be what we think they ought to be (which is generally "like us"). (Attempting to change another person and control what they do is using power over, down against them. It is a form of violence.) Without healthy boundaries, we do for them what they could and should do for themselves. Rather than helping them, we hurt them by keeping them in a position of dependency. They never learn to be self-responsible and, thus, never grow up emotionally-relationally-spiritually. Healthy boundaries help us use our power to authentically serve the other by empowering them and nurturing their growth. Healthy boundaries are a prerequisite to serving in life-giving, life-enhancing ways. (For an explanation of healthy boundaries in relationships, see Chapters 18 & 19 in my book <u>Discovering Your True Self: A Guide for the Journey</u>.)

63. See again Exodus 34:6—7 where these three ways of dealing with human sin are specifically identified as a part of the LORD's merciful and gracious character.

64. See Romans 1:18—32.

65. Our inclination to portray God as angry and judging is a projection of our response to wrong rather than God's. Anger expressed in condemnation, judgment, and punishment is how we humans typically react to the wrongdoing of others. This reaction is seen in how Moses reacted to the building and worshipping of the golden calf by the Israelites at Mt. Sinai (Exodus 32). It is opposite of the way the LORD deals with human sin as expressed in the revelation of the divine character in Exodus 34. For a more detailed development of the Exodus 32—34 text, see my book <u>God's Plumb Line: Aligning Our Hearts with the Heart of God</u>.

66. Such pyramid-type towers have been used in many cultures as places of worship. The Aztecs, Incas, and Egyptians built pyramids. Ancient Babylon built ziggurats.

67. See again FN 44 and Job 1:6; 2:1.

68. See again Chapter 1.

Printed in the United States
by Baker & Taylor Publisher Services